UNSUNG
HER**O**ES
(and a Few Villains)

WANDA ROBINSON

GOSPEL
ADVOCATE

A TRUSTED NAME SINCE 1855

Published by Gospel Advocate Co.
1006 Elm Hill Pike, Nashville, TN 37210
www.gospeladvocate.com

ISBN: 978-0-89225-660-0

Introduction

We are all familiar with the giants of Scripture: Abraham, Joseph, David, Peter, Stephen, Paul, but what about those men whose names and stories are mentioned only briefly in Scripture? Much can be learned from a study of these lesser known men in the Bible – the unsung heroes, if you will – that can enrich our lives.

You may recognize the names of Boaz, Ishmael and Caleb because they are featured in Bible passages you have studied; however, we are going to be looking at these men and others from their perspectives instead of that of the main characters in the narratives. We will also look for connections and facts you may not have noticed previously. Other names in this study may be unfamiliar to you such as Ithamar, Ebed-Melech and Gehazi. Because the Holy Spirit directed that events from their lives be recorded for us, they also are appropriate subjects for our study. Open your Bibles, and let's take a new look at these men of old.

Wanda Robinson

Dedication

Dedicated to my dear husband, Wendell, who assisted me with his encouraging words and much utilized red ink pen, and to the beautiful ladies in the Sunday and Wednesday Bible classes who continually lift me up.

Table of
CONTENTS

1. **Ishmael** – Living in a Dysfunctional Family 9

2. **Hur** – Playing a Supporting Role 17

3. **Ithamar** – List-Making Extraordinaire 23

4. **Caleb** – Don't Go With the Flow 31

5. **Korah** – Mutiny on the Desert 39

6. **Achan** – Caught Red-Handed 47

7. **Boaz** – A True Gentleman 55

8. **Nabal's Servant** – Standing Up and Speaking Out ... 63

9. **450 Prophets of Baal** – Wild and Crazy Guys 69

10. **Gehazi** – A Servant Who Desired Riches 77

11. **The Man Who Touched Elisha's Bones** –
    A Second Chance at Life 85

12. **King Manasseh** – The Boy Who Wore a Crown 93

13. **Ebed-Melech** – Beyond the Call of Duty 101

ISHMAEL:
Living in a Dysfunctional Family

Genesis 16; 17; 21:9-21; 25:7-18; 28:9

Her mom was a drug addict; her dad was a drug addict – even her grandmother was hooked on drugs. At age 13, Susie (not her real name) started doing drugs as well; before long, she was also an addict. For the next 10 years, she was "high" more often than not. As a teenager, she started racking up arrests and going to jail. As soon as she was released from jail, she would look for her next high. Cocaine was her favorite drug. Once, her mother picked her up when she was released from jail and drove her straight to her drug dealer's house; she was strung out on drugs within 30 minutes. On one brief "vacation" from jail, she spent six days with no food and no sleep – just drugs. I had known Susie briefly when she was just a little girl, but I saw her again in the local jail while I was working with our jail ministry. As we talked about her drug habit, she admitted, "I don't know how to live sober."

We studied the Scriptures together for a few weeks. Finally, Susie was able to go to yet another rehab center, but this time, she had a new determination to make it work – and she did! Susie worked hard to understand her addiction and to learn how to break free. She finally realized she needed to get away from the bad influences in her life, including her mother and friends, if she was ever going to be whole and healthy again. When she completed drug rehab, she moved away, got a job and started attending Narcotics Anonymous classes. About a year later, Susie surprised me with a visit. She was doing great. She was sober and healthy; she not only still had a job but had gotten a promotion. Susie admitted that she didn't know life could be like this. She told me, "You tried to tell me, but I just didn't understand."

Susie did not have a pleasant upbringing, living in a dysfunctional family with family members who had problems of their own. She could have given up and blamed her struggles as an adult on her bad upbringing. Instead she worked to make her life better, overcoming the trials of her childhood to become a sober, productive young woman. Sadly, millions of adults have stories similar to Susie's because childhood is not always the fairy tale we wish it to be. A difficult childhood, however, does not give us an excuse to live a life not pleasing to God.

We read of a man in the Bible who also had a difficult childhood. His family was fractured, and he often didn't know the direction his life was headed. His troubles started when his parents wanted to have a baby. Abram and Sarai longed for a child, but it just wasn't happening. They were about to run out of time. After all, Abram was 86 and Sarai was 76. When we consider their longer life spans, this would probably be the equivalent to our being in our 40s. Finally, in desperation, Sarai gave her Egyptian maidservant Hagar to Abraham as a concubine (Genesis 16:1-2). A concubine was a woman with whom a man could legally have sexual relations; she was not really a wife, but she was considered a member of the family.[1] This sounds strange to our ears, but it was common in ancient times to solve the problem of barrenness by using a slave woman as a surrogate.[2]

Hagar became pregnant, but her attitude toward her mistress Sarai drastically changed: "her mistress became despised in her eyes" (Genesis 16:4). Why do you think this happened? Verse 4 in the Easy-to-Read Version says: "She became very proud and began to feel that she was better than Sarai her owner." "Ha! I got pregnant, and you didn't" may have been her attitude. Sarai obviously didn't like it and treated Hagar harshly, causing her to run away to the desert. There, an angel of the Lord told Hagar to return to Sarai and submit to her. The angel also told her she would have a son (more accurate than an ultrasound) and that she should call him Ishmael (v. 11) which means "God hears."[3]

Ishmael would be a wild donkey of a man, untamed and free. Hagar returned to her mistress and bore a son whom Abram named Ishmael.

Ishmael was reared as the son of Abram but also as the son of Hagar, an Egyptian servant. He still was considered a slave. As Ishmael neared his 13th birthday, his life suddenly was about to go in a different direction. Abram was now 99 years old. The Lord appeared to him and told him that he would be the father of a multitude of nations. God wanted to establish a covenant or agreement with Abram that He would be their God and his family would be God's people. The proof of this pledge would be the circumcision of every male in the family. Then God changed their names from Abram to Abraham and from Sarai to Sarah (Genesis 17:5, 15). But God had even more astonishing news; He told him that Sarah would bear Abraham a son. Abraham could not help laughing to himself, for Sarah was 90 years old. (I am pretty sure I would have cried at that news!) Verse 18 tells us, "And Abraham said to God, 'Oh, that Ishmael might live before You!' " Abraham evidently thought that Ishmael was the son God had previously promised who would establish his descendants (15:4-5). That error was quickly corrected when God promised that Sarah herself would bear a son and his name would be Isaac (16:19). Abraham was assured that Ishmael would also be blessed and would be the father of a great nation (v. 20), but Isaac was the one with whom God would establish His covenant. When God left, Abraham, Ishmael and all the men in the household were circumcised, just as God had commanded (v. 23).

So Ishmael was going to be a big brother. Anytime a new baby comes into a home, changes take place in the family dynamics, and this family was no different. Just as the Lord had promised, Sarah became pregnant and gave birth to a son. Can you imagine how joyful she must have been to finally hold her own baby in her arms at the age of 90? As was customary among the Hebrew children, Sarah nursed her son until he was ready to be weaned at about the age of 3 or 4.[4] Because the weaning of a young child was a big deal, Abraham threw a great feast to celebrate (Genesis 21:8).

Ishmael at this time would have been 16 or 17 years old. Is anyone familiar with the attitudes of teenagers? They are not always pleasant. "And Sarah saw the son of Hagar the Egyptian, whom she had borne to Abraham, scoffing" (Genesis 21:9). Various versions say the son of Hagar was poking fun, mocking, playing or laughing. Whatever he was doing, Sarah didn't like it. It seemed his behavior spoiled the party for her. She insisted that Ishmael and his mother be sent away. No longer was Sarah content to raise Ishmael and Isaac in the same household. Abraham was upset and reluctant to expel his son from his tents. Remember that Ishmael had been raised as Abraham's only son for 13 years before the birth of Isaac; Abraham did not want to disown or hurt this son in any way. God graciously again appeared to Abraham to calm his troubled heart, telling Abraham to do as Sarah asked.

Abraham did as God told him and sent away Hagar and Ishmael with only some bread and a skin of water. Once again Hagar, this time accompanied by her son Ishmael, sought refuge in the desert. What a sad situation. Once their food and water ran out, they found themselves in the desert with no home, no money, no food, no water and no hope. Hagar knew she could not bear to watch her son die of thirst in the heat of the sun. She had him sit in the shade of a shrub while she walked a distance away to keep from seeing him suffer in his final moments of life. Then she sat down and cried.

God is not blind to His children's pain. Someone said, "Don't worry. God is never blind to your tears, never deaf to your prayers, and never silent to your pain. He sees, He hears and He will deliver." [5] For a second time, deliverance from God came to Hagar in the wilderness. Isn't it interesting that we are told Hagar was weeping, but God heard the cries of Ishmael (Genesis 21:16-17)? God sent an angel to reassure Hagar of God's care. God had not forgotten His promise to make of Ishmael a great nation, and God assured Hagar that this would be accomplished. As the first step toward that goal, God provided water for their immediate need by opening her eyes to see a nearby well (v. 19). Have you ever been really, really thirsty? Not just, "I think I will get a glass of water" thirsty, but "My mouth feels like cotton" thirsty? How refreshing that first sip of water would have been to the parched mouths of Ishmael and Hagar. In that single drink of water, hope must have been restored to their hearts.

God did not choose to tell us what happened in the next chapter of Ishmael's life. We are not told the day-to-day details of his adult years nor what became of Hagar. We are told, however, what is most important – that God was with Ishmael. God kept His promise to Hagar to bless this son of Abraham. Ishmael settled in that same Wilderness of Paran, between Canaan and the mountains of Sinai. He became an archer, and he took a wife from the land of Egypt (Genesis 21:20-21). Ishmael became the father of a great host of people. Genesis 25:13-15 records the names of the 12 sons of Ishmael. His descendants consisted of many Arab nations including the Ishmaelites whom we read of several times throughout Scripture (Genesis 37:24-28; 39:1; Judges 8:24; Psalm 83:6). Ishmael also had a daughter who became the bride of Esau when Esau realized his father wanted him to marry someone from their family (Genesis 28:8-9); obviously the relatives had stayed in touch over the years.

The only other time we see Ishmael is at the burial of Abraham (Genesis 25:7-10). How interesting to see these two brothers unite for the funeral of their father. Considering their somewhat rocky past and the fact that they were not even part of the same household after Isaac was just a toddler, it is amazing that they came together to pay honor to Abraham after his death. This may be an indication that Ishmael lived not too far from Abraham as the burial usually took place within a few hours after death.[6] Ishmael himself died at the age of 137 (v. 17), but his descendants continued to be adversaries of his brother's people long after his death.

What Lessons Do We Learn From the Life of Ishmael?

1. Life is not fair.

Ishmael really did not get a fair break. It wasn't his fault that Sarai decided to give Hagar to Abram to have a baby; it wasn't his fault that Abram and Sarai were eventually blessed by God with his little brother who was the promised child of the covenant. It wasn't really his fault, although his behavior could have been a little better, that he and his mother were tossed out of their home. Ishmael had to learn quickly as a teenager that life is not fair. I suspect when they left the protection of Abraham that Ishmael had to grow up quickly and be "the man of the tent." Has anything bad ever happened to you that made you believe life is not fair? Maybe you lost your job because of budget cuts; perhaps you tried to be a good wife, but your husband left you for a younger woman; or you had just paid off your credit card bill and then your car died. A friend of mine unexpectedly received a gift of $500; the next day she discovered her house had termites. Not fair!

When Joseph refused to commit adultery with Potiphar's wife, he was thrown into prison. That was not fair (Genesis 39:6-20). When Balaam's donkey kept him from being killed by the angel in the path three times, the poor donkey was beaten for it each time. That was not fair (Numbers 22:22-33). Certainly it was proof that life is not fair when Stephen was stoned to death for his faith in Jesus Christ (Acts 7:58-60). Sometimes we have to just accept that life is not fair.

2. We must not let a difficult childhood keep us from living a life pleasing to God.

Certainly, this is easier said than done. Ishmael was kicked out of the only home he knew when he was about 16 years old. I suspect living around Sarah and Hagar was not always a bed of roses either.

Our experiences throughout our early lives undoubtedly contribute to our attitudes, behaviors and beliefs as adults, but if our early days were not as carefree as we would have wished, we must put that behind us and press on to living in a way God would want. Remember what Paul said in Philippians 3:13-14: "Brethren, I do not count myself to have apprehended; but one thing I do, forgetting those things which are behind and reaching forward to those things which are ahead, I press toward the goal for the prize of the upward call of God in Christ Jesus." Using an unpleasant childhood as an excuse for bad behavior as an adult will not be acceptable to God.

3. You have to play the hand you are dealt.

We can't trade cards with someone else; we can't refuse to play if we don't like our cards. The cards we are dealt are the cards we must play. Some people are born into this world with a good playing hand: a happy family, good health, plenty of money. Others are dealt a much worse hand that includes such adversities as poverty, a broken home or child abuse. We cannot change those cards; we must play them in the very best way we can. Even the philosopher Voltaire, born in 1694, wrote: "Each player must accept the cards life deals him or her: but once they are in hand, he or she alone must decide how to play the cards in order to win the game." [7] It is up to us to decide whether we are going to let the hardships of life overcome us or whether we will be faithful Christians in spite of the adversities that life throws at us.

Yet in all these things we are more than conquerors through Him who loved us. (Romans 8:37)

With God on our side, there is nothing life can throw at us that we cannot overcome.

Ishmael was not destined to be the promised son. His time on this earth was not filled with ease and luxury, but he seemed to live his life as well as he could, becoming the father of many nations and living to an old age. Perhaps the best lesson we can learn from Ishmael is to accept our lot in life and deal with it the best way possible. We have the advantage of knowing that we are blessed with God's loving care and that He will help us no matter our plight on this earth.

Let's Think About This

1. Why would the Jews desire so strongly to have children?

2. How old do you think Hagar might have been?

3. As the son of the slave woman Hagar, Ishmael would have also been considered a slave even though he was the son of his master Abraham. How do you think this would have made Ishmael feel?

4. Put yourself in Abraham's place. What do you think Abraham expected to happen to Hagar and Ishmael once their food and water ran out? What might Abraham have said to Ishmael before sending him away?

5. How might the rejection by Abraham have affected Ishmael?

6. What parable refers to another celebration that was disrupted by the attitude of an older brother?

7. What suggestions can you offer on how to overcome a difficult childhood?

HUR:
Playing a Supporting Role

Exodus 17:8-13; 24:12-15

F amous people gather each year in Hollywood for a lavish celebration of the best actors and actresses in recent movies. Expensive designer gowns and tuxedos are bought; diamond jewelry is selected. Everyone nervously awaits the opening of the secret envelopes to see who will walk away with the prized statuettes. The first Academy Awards ceremony was held in 1929 and lasted only 15 minutes. Today, the ceremony is held in Dolby Theatre with 3,300 people attending and is broadcast worldwide. Best Actor in a Supporting Role is one of the four top individual awards. The man who holds the record for the most wins in that category with three Oscars is Walter Brennan, remembered by many of us as being famous in his later years for playing crusty old sidekicks in Western movies.[1]

Many of us are called on to play supporting roles throughout our lives, but none more so than a man in the Old Testament named Hur, who is first mentioned in the book of Exodus. Hur is one among the tens of thousands of Israelites wandering in the wilderness after their recent escape from Egypt, but we know little of his background. Hur was a common name during Bible times; with several men by the name of Hur mentioned in Scripture, it is sometimes difficult to differentiate which one is which. This Hur seemingly was from the tribe of Judah (1 Chronicles 2:19). It is possible that this man named Hur was the son of Caleb who would later faithfully spy out the land of Canaan. According to tradition and to the words of Josephus, the historian, (Ant, III, ii, 4:vi, 1) Hur was the husband of Miriam, which would make him the brother-in-law of Moses. Nothing in Scripture confirms that.[2] We do know that he was evidently a trusted official among the Israelites.

The Israelites had just started their long journey through the wilderness after leaving Egypt when they were suddenly attacked by an army of Amalekites trying to obstruct their passage. The Israelites were evidently coming into the region inhabited by the Amalekites, but Bible scholars are unsure of the exact location of Rephidim (Exodus 17:8). It is thought that the Amalekites, a nomadic or wandering people, were descendants from Abraham through Esau and his grandson Amalek.[3] We do know that the Amalekites remained bitter enemies of the Israelites throughout the Old Testament. When faced with the invading forces, Moses directed Joshua to field an army of carefully selected men and engage in battle with the enemy. In the meantime, Moses went atop a hill where he could watch the skirmish and perhaps direct the battle by using his staff to signal where the soldiers should deploy.[4]

The next day Joshua led the men in battle as Moses arrived at the top of the hill where he could keep an eye on the fighting. With Moses were his brother Aaron as well as Hur. The battle was fierce and long as Joshua commanded the soldiers in fighting against the Amalekites while Moses oversaw the battle from the hilltop. I have always been impressed with hair stylists and the way they hold their arms up working with hair all day long. How tiring that must be. Moses had to hold his arms up like that. Standing high above the battle, he could see where the Amalekites were stationed and which direction the Israelite soldiers should proceed in order to advance. Moses probably managed the battle with his staff from his vantage point, pointing the staff in the direction the soldiers should go. When his arms were holding up the staff and the soldiers could see his instructions, they were winning the battle; but when he lowered his arms from fatigue, the Amalekites were able to gain the advantage.

Hur and Aaron stepped in to help; they could see what was happening and came up with a plan. First, Hur and Aaron found a stone to act as a seat for Moses. When he sat down, they stood, one on each side, and held his hands up for him. Hur and Aaron continued to support Moses all day, "until the going down of the sun" (Exodus 17:12), and the Israelites won the battle. In Deuteronomy 25:17-19 we read of the long-term result of this conflict.

This is not all we are told about Hur. We see him again in a supporting role in Exodus 24:12-15. Moses not only acted as a leader but also as a judge for the people (18:13). Per God's command, Moses made several trips up Mount Sinai, and each expedition lasted several weeks. This meant he had to leave someone in charge while he was meeting with God. On this occasion, he chose his brother Aaron and the faithful Hur to take on this enormous responsibility (24:14). Moses entrusted them with the well-being of the Israelite nation; they were to take his place in making judgments regarding the people until he returned.

What Lessons Do We Learn From Hur?

1. Hur was called upon to play a supporting role rather than to lead.

Hur knew that he was not the leader of the Israelites, and he didn't try to take over that position even when Moses needed help. Hur didn't try to take the staff and hold it up himself; he didn't try to talk Moses out of holding up his arms. He simply did the best he could to support Moses in a difficult situation.

We may be called on to play a supporting role rather than a lead one. This is a hard lesson for some people to learn. Have you ever known anyone who was upset because he or she wasn't asked to head up a project? On the old *Gomer Pyle U.S.M.C.* TV show, Gomer's sergeant wanted him to try his hand at leading the platoon. Gomer refused, saying, "I'm no good at leadership. Now, followship, I'm real good at that." Where would this world be if everyone was a leader and no one wanted to follow? How much work would get done in the church if people only wanted to participate in a good work if they could be the leader? We must be willing to work in a supporting role if needed.

2. Hur served in a tiring job.

Do you suppose Hur's arms got tired while they were holding up the hand of Moses? Sure. Was it boring? Maybe. But he didn't stop; instead he stayed steady at his post until the battle was over.

Unsung Heroes (and a Few Villains)

We may be asked to do a tiring job. Teaching classes can be tiring; working in a benevolent program sorting clothes can be physically demanding; cooking for Meals-on-Wheels can be exhausting. Some jobs are required to be done only once; other jobs have to be done repeatedly. The Scriptures encourage us to renew our strength when weariness threatens to overtake us.

Come to Me, all you who labor and are heavy laden, and I will give you rest. (Matthew 11:28)

And let us not grow weary while doing good, for in due season we shall reap if we do not lose heart. (Galatians 6:9)

But as for you, brethren, do not grow weary in doing good. (2 Thessalonians 3:13)

For consider Him who endured such hostility from sinners against Himself, lest you become weary and discouraged in your souls. (Hebrews 12:3)

3. Moses, Aaron and Hur all had to do their part.

What if Aaron had let one of Moses' hands down, or what if Moses refused to allow Aaron and Hur to help him? If Hur had decided that holding up the arm of Moses only halfway was good enough, the story might have had a different ending. Each man had to fulfill his specific task.

We need to do our part as well, for the Lord's work takes all of us functioning together. Have you ever heard anyone say, "Someone else can do that better than me," or "I have done enough; it is someone else's turn"? Perhaps you have even said something like that yourself. We are very familiar with the passage in 1 Corinthians 12:14-24 regarding the different parts of the body working together in harmony. Verses 25-27 in the Easy-to-Read Version read: "God did this so that our body would not be divided. God wanted the different parts to care the same for each other. If one part of the body suffers, then all the other parts suffer with it. Or if one part is honored, then all the other parts share its honor. All of you together are the body of Christ. Each one of you is a part of that body." As Christians, we need to work together in unity, and each one of us has to participate. Like Hur, we need to do what we can to further the cause of Christ,

20

whether it is holding up the hand of someone else who is working or doing the job ourselves.

4. Hur had the trust of Moses.

At this time, the Israelites included thousands of men Moses could have chosen to accompany him to the hilltop as well as to put in charge of the people in his absence, and he chose Hur. Evidently Hur had demonstrated to Moses that he was reliable and trustworthy, and Moses knew that he could depend on him.

As Christian women, we need to be trustworthy. Our reputation needs to be that of women who are both honorable and reliable. Do you know people you are hesitant to call on to do something because you don't trust them? They are always late; they fail to finish anything; they do everything in a careless manner; they speak when they should be silent. I am reminded of people who signed up to work at vacation Bible school and then just never showed up or people who volunteer to do a job and then do it in a half-hearted manner. Do other people trust you? Have you proven yourself to be dependable?

Hur did his part by working tirelessly and faithfully in a supporting role. Hur gets my vote for "Best Supporter" in the Scriptures. We don't know much about the man named Hur, but what little we do know shows him to be a faithful and trustworthy servant of God. He is certainly worthy of our respect and imitation.

Let's Think About This

1. Do you consider yourself a leader or a follower? In what ways do you strive to do the best you can in either role?

2. In what specific ways can we support our leaders in the church?

3. How can we motivate ourselves to do the Lord's work when we are tired?

4. What characteristics come to mind when you hear the word "trustworthy"? Can the elders of the church trust you to carry out the Lord's work?

5. What other people in the Bible played supporting roles?

ITHAMAR:
List-Maker Extraordinaire
Exodus 38:21; Leviticus 10:1-7, 12-20

J eanne Robertson is a Christian humorist who travels the country
entertaining audiences. She tells the hilarious story about wanting
to make a pound cake for a sick friend. Jeanne asked her husband
to go to the grocery store to buy the ingredients to bake the cake. He was
in a hurry, but she promised him the list would be short so he could go
through the speedy checkout lane. She wrote out a grocery list for him
and he followed it perfectly. Unfortunately, she numbered the items on
the list, so it read, "1. pound of butter; 2. large bottle vanilla flavoring;
3. dozen eggs; 4. big tub of shortening; 5. 5 lb. bag sugar; 6. 5 lb. bag
all-purpose flour; and 7. 6-pack of lemon-lime soda." You guessed it: He
bought one pound of margarine, two large bottles of vanilla flavoring,
three dozen eggs, four big tubs of shortening, five bags of sugar, six bags
of all-purpose flour, and seven 6-packs of lemon-lime soda. That would
make a lot of pound cakes![1]

I am a list-maker, and I make no apologies for it. I keep a running
to-do list of things I need to accomplish, including a daily to-do list
and a long-term to-do list of things I will get to eventually; I have
a prayer list; I make shopping lists; I keep a Christmas list going
all year long; I have a list of authors I like; I have a list of ideas for
Bible lessons; I even have a list of what my husband likes on his sub
sandwich. As a result of my list-making tendencies, I have a new

Bible hero, a man who was assigned a special job – to make a list.

This list-maker's name was Ithamar and he was the fourth and youngest son of Aaron, making him the nephew of Moses (Exodus 28:1). The name Ithamar means "island of the palm-tree."[2] According to God's wishes, Aaron became the high priest of the Israelites and his sons would serve as priests under him; they would wear the priestly garments and serve in the tabernacle. This arrangement worked out well for a while; however, a time came when two of Ithamar's brothers disobeyed the Lord.

When offering incense, Nadab and Abihu used a "profane fire" before the Lord (Leviticus 10:1). Although the meaning of this strange fire is not clear, it is possible it was fire taken from some source other than the perpetual fire that was to be kept burning on the altar (6:13). There is no doubt, however, that Nadab and Abihu did not follow the Lord's directions concerning the burning of this incense, for fire came down from the Lord and destroyed them both. Can you imagine this scene? Everything is peaceful and calm one minute as they are worshiping God, and the next moment two men are on the ground dead (10:2). The words of Moses precluded any objection regarding their deaths that might have been made by Aaron. He was not even permitted to grieve for his sons. Priests were expected to respect God and His laws, and because Nadab and Abihu disobeyed, punishment followed. Aaron had to accept God's judgment.

Eleazar and Ithamar were also not allowed to mourn their brothers' deaths (Leviticus 10:6). Grief was generally expressed by weeping loudly, tearing one's clothes, wearing sackcloth, shaving the head or beard and fasting, but the remaining brothers were to do none of these things. Eleazar and Ithamar still had to carry out their responsibilities as priests. They were forbidden to grieve the deaths of those who had failed to honor God (v. 7).

There is an interesting sidebar in Leviticus 10:16-18. Moses is angry with Eleazar and Ithamar. Aaron had earlier sacrificed a goat for a sin offering for the people (9:15). According to the law, if the blood of the sin offering was brought into the holy place, the flesh was to be burnt outside the camp, otherwise the meat was to be eaten by the priests in the holy place (6:24-30). In this instance, the blood of the goat was not brought into the holy place, and yet it seems that the flesh was burned outside the camp instead of being eaten by the priests. Because this was so soon after the Lord's judgment on Nadab and Abihu, it seems Moses wanted the Law to be followed explicitly. He therefore rebuked Eleazar and Ithamar on this account, but their father, Aaron, spoke up in their defense (10:19).

It is possible that Aaron directed his sons to burn the goat outside the camp because he was the one who answered Moses' reprimand. Basically Aaron said that he could not eat the offering in good conscience considering what had just happened; he was afraid the Lord would not accept this worship when his heart was so full of sorrow instead of joy (Deuteronomy 12:7). Eating the sin offering should correspond with a time of celebration and feasting, but Aaron, Eleazar and Ithamar just didn't feel like rejoicing after witnessing their loved ones killed. Their hearts were full of grief. Moses seemed to accept this answer. We don't read of any further scolding (Leviticus 10:20).

As the next oldest living brother, Eleazar was eventually appointed high priest, succeeding Aaron (Numbers 20:27-28). Ithamar remained a priest and had responsibilities assigned to him; he was to be in charge of two families in the service of the tabernacle (Numbers 4:21-33). Ithamar had one other job as well; he was to keep a list. Exodus 38:21 reads this way in the Easy-to-Read Version: "Moses commanded the Levites to write down everything that was used to make the Holy Tent, that is, the Tent of the Agreement. Ithamar, son of Aaron was in charge of keeping the list." Paul was a tent-maker; Ithamar was a list-maker.

Ithamar's family remained common priests until the time that his descendant Eli was appointed high priest, although we are not told why that happened. Later the high priesthood was taken away from Ithamar's family and returned to the descendants of his brother Eleazar's family (1 Kings 2:27, 35).[3] That is all we are told about Ithamar.

What Lessons Do We Learn From Ithamar?

1. Ithamar continued to serve God in the midst of personal sorrow.

We think of Job as one who continued to be loyal to God even though he lost his family and material possessions. Ithamar saw two of his brothers struck down right in front of him by the hand of God, but he also persisted in his obedience to God Almighty. Some people question God when bad things happen, asking, "Why did this terrible thing happen to me?" Others blame God for their troubles and decide to abandon their faith completely; some people neglect God because they are so engulfed by their grief. They abandon the worship services; they stop personal Bible study; they fail to pray. Ithamar continued performing his duties as a priest even immediately after his brothers' deaths. He did not forsake God or his service to Him.

2. Ithamar took on great responsibilities for the Lord.

This was no small task considering how many men between the ages of 30 and 50 were counted. The Gershonites had 2,630 men, and the Merari family had 3,200 for a total of 5,830 workers that Ithamar was to supervise (Numbers 4:21-45). Ithamar performed the function of a priest as well as making sure these workers were fulfilling their duties in the tabernacle. Ithamar was assigned a job that required dependability and accountability.

3. Ithamar worked according to God's will.

Under God's direction, Moses had ordered that everything in the tabernacle be listed; Ithamar carried out this huge job. An accounting of all the offerings for the building of the tabernacle was to be kept. The estimate for materials used in construction of the tabernacle included nearly a ton of gold, about 3.25 tons of silver, and 2.25 tons of bronze.[4] An accurate report of such massive amounts would require organization and reliability.

As I have been doing my daily Bible reading, I have been struck by how many lists are in the Scriptures. Some lists quickly come to mind, including the Ten Commandments, the fruit of the Spirit, and lists of apostles – but there are many more. First Chronicles is full of lists of Israelite families as well as lists of David's mighty men. The book of Ezra lists items brought from the Lord's temple when they returned from Babylon as well as multiple lists of family members who returned from exile. Nehemiah numbers not only the descendants of various Israelites in Jerusalem but also has lists of singers, gatekeepers and temple servants. In Proverbs 6:16-19 Solomon gives us a list of seven things the Lord hates. Galatians 5:19-21 gives us the works of the flesh in list form. First Timothy records the characteristics an elder should possess as well as the requirements for a woman to be added to the list of widows. The writers of the Scriptures were directed by the Holy Spirit to supply these lists for our benefit.

Whatever method we use to stay organized, whether making lists or using some other means, we need to remember that our God is a God of peace, not chaos (1 Thessalonians 5:23). Five times in Scripture God is referred to as "the God of peace." We don't see a harried God in the Scriptures, running here and there, never getting anything done. God doesn't want our lives to be wrapped in frenzy; He wants us to experience His peace. The fruit of the Spirit include peace, gentleness and self-control (Galatians 5:22-23), attributes that do not lend themselves to a life of hectic confusion. Perhaps learning to be a list-maker will help us stay calm and focus more on God and pleasing Him.

First Corinthians 14:33 refers to worship, but the premise is valid in other parts of our lives: "For God is not the author of confusion but of peace, as in all the churches of the saints."

Our God is not a God of confusion. In *Barnes' Notes*, we read: "His (God's) religion cannot tend to produce disorder. He is the God of peace; and his religion will tend to promote order. It is calm, peaceful, thoughtful. It is not boisterous and disorderly."[5]

"Dear Lord and Father of Mankind" is a hymn we often sing. The beautiful words of that song were taken from a poem, *The Brewing of Soma*, written by American poet John Greenleaf Whittier in 1872.[6] The words of one particular verse can help us to focus on the peacefulness that can be ours as we think of our Creator and Master. "Drop Thy still dews of quietness, / Till all our strivings cease; / Take from our souls the strain and stress, / And let our ordered lives confess / The beauty of Thy peace."

If our lives are chaotic, perhaps we need to slow down, get organized and focus on the God of peace. We need to continue our service to God no matter what may be going on in our lives; we need to take responsibility for the work of the Lord, doing whatever we can to serve Him; and we need to do it all according to God's will, even if that means making lists like Ithamar.

Let's Think About This

1. Do you know people who have let personal tragedy turn them away from God? How can we help them come back to God?

2. Why was it important to keep a list of everything used for the tabernacle?

3. What lists other than those mentioned in this lesson can you find in the Scriptures?

4. What keeps us from having a sense of peace?

5. Is your life one of calm or of chaos? How can you become more peaceful in your day-to-day life?

How Can Lists Help Us Navigate Our Busy Lives?

1. Lists bring order to chaos.

Life can truly be overwhelming at times. We have so much to do involving family, work, home, friends and the church. Sometimes we are left to wonder how we can ever get it all done. Instead of the bedlam that ensues when we are running from one project to the next before finishing the first one, we can organize our tasks and even prioritize them. You may have heard the true story about a consultant, Ivy Lee, who was challenged by Charles Schwab, president of Bethlehem Steel. Schwab agreed to pay anything within reason if Lee could show him a way to get more things done with his time. The plan Lee came up with consisted of writing down the most important tasks that needed to be done the next day and numbering them in order of importance. Then the next morning Schwab would begin on No. 1 and finish it; then begin on No. 2; then No. 3 and so on. Schwab later wrote his consultant a check for $25,000, saying this was the most profitable lesson he had ever learned.[7]

2. Lists give us a sense of peace.

Did you know that just the act of making a list of all we need to accomplish helps us be more productive? We feel more in control and more peaceful when we write everything down.

3. Lists keep us focused.

Let's face it; we are forgetful. We have good intentions, but we get so busy that we forget some things. It is hard to keep our minds on track when we have so many responsibilities, so many things to remember. Have you ever started to write some checks, but then remembered that you needed to return a phone call? By the time you made your phone call, you realized you needed to start supper. When you went to the kitchen, you decided to clean out the refrigerator. Somehow you never got back to writing checks. If we have a list of all those things we are supposed to do, we can concentrate on each item and get it done. Lists help us stay focused on the jobs at hand.

4. Lists give us a sense of accomplishment.

It feels great to mark something off a list. When we have completed a task and scribble through that line on the list, we experience a sense of achievement. We are encouraged to continue other tasks.

CALEB:
Don't Go With the Flow

Numbers 13–14; 34:16-19; Joshua 14:6-13; 15:13-19;
1 Chronicles 2:18-19

I n 1847 a medical doctor named Ignaz Philipp Semmelweis, who was assistant director at the Vienna Maternity Hospital, suggested to the doctors that the high rate of deaths of patients and new babies was due to the fact that the doctors attending them were carrying infections from the diseased and dead people they had previously touched. Semmelweis ordered doctors to wash their hands with soap and water and rinse them in a strong chemical before examining their patients. He tried to get doctors to wear clean clothes, and he battled for clean wards; however, the majority of doctors disagreed with Semmelweis, and they deliberately disobeyed his orders.[1] In the late 19th century, on the basis of the work by Semmelweis, Joseph Lister began soaking surgery instruments, the operating table, his hands and the patients with carbolic acid with astonishing results. What was previously risky surgery now became routine. However, the majority of doctors criticized his work also.[2] Today we know that Lister and Semmelweis were right; the majority of doctors in their day were wrong. Just because the majority believes something does not necessarily mean it is true.

It is sometimes hard to stand with the minority, especially when the minority consists of only two people. Caleb found himself in that same position. Caleb was with the Israelites when they left Egypt and headed toward the Promised Land, but surprisingly enough, he was evidently not born an Israelite. In Joshua 14:14 Caleb is called "the son of Jephunneh the

Kenizzite." Although we do not have any information about the Kenizzites, we do know from Genesis 36:15 that they were descendants of Esau and not Jacob (from whom the Israelites descended). *Nelson's Illustrated Bible Dictionary* explains that many of the tribes of Israel included people outside the ties of blood kinship. These were people who had become associated with the group through conversion, marriage, adoption or slavery.[3] Caleb most likely merged with the tribe of Judah through one of these means and developed faith in God. Later he is listed as being a leader of the tribe of Judah and head of the Hezronite family (Numbers 13:6).

When we first meet Caleb, he is 40 years old and has just been chosen for an important mission. The Israelites have been traveling for approximately a year after their exodus from Egypt and are on the verge of finally entering the land of Canaan. Before they can set foot in the Promised Land, however, God told Moses to send in 12 spies to check out the land so they would know what they were up against. Caleb, Joshua, and 10 other men were hand-picked for this task. Their assignment was simple. They were to see what the land was like, whether the people who lived in it were strong or weak and whether they were few or many. They were also to check out the land to see if it was good for growing crops and to check out the cities and report back to Moses. The question we might ask is why they had to spy out the land at all. God had already told them everything they needed to know about Canaan. It was a land flowing with milk and honey and was promised to them by God. What else mattered? Perhaps God wanted them to determine the best strategy for overtaking the land, but that is not how it turned out.

The spies were gone for 40 days, after which they returned to their home base and were ready to give a report to all the people of what they had discovered. But their report was surely not the report the people were expecting. The spies described fruit that was huge and delicious-looking, but the land was crawling with enemies. They said they saw giants and "[they] were like grasshoppers" compared to the natives (Numbers 13:33). The Israelites were terrified. Remember, this generation of Israelites had known only a life of slavery in Egypt. What did they know about fighting or going to battle against an enemy? They were slaves, not soldiers.

Caleb tried to calm the people and reassure them that they could overtake this land. All the spies saw the same land, the same crops and the same inhabitants, but their conclusions were different. Allen Webster in his tract *Why Caleb Lived on a Mountain* writes: "The others couldn't see God for the giants; Caleb couldn't see the giants for God." Sadly, Caleb and Joshua were outnumbered as the Israelites listened to the negative report from the 10 spies and became afraid and discouraged. The people were frightened and thought that even slavery in Egypt was preferable to fighting these giants. They had quickly forgotten that God had parted the Red Sea, fed them with manna and provided water from a rock when they were thirsty. They were so upset that they were ready to desert Moses who had led them so courageously the previous several months. Caleb and Joshua tried once more to insert a voice of reason.

Only do not rebel against the LORD, nor fear the people of the land, for they are our bread; their protection has departed from them, and the LORD is with us. Do not fear them. (Numbers 14:9)

Caleb and Joshua tore their clothes as a sign of their distress and pleaded with the Israelites to trust the Lord, insisting that He would protect them if they would just let Him, but the Israelites were having no part of it. Instead, they wanted to stone Caleb and Joshua in order to silence them. Caleb and Joshua, however, were proven right in believing God would protect them, for He did.

"The glory of the LORD appeared" saving the two men from the fury of the people (Numbers 14:10). The phrase, "glory of the Lord," is used frequently in Scripture, but it is still hard for us to imagine. The term often refers to a brightness or a cloud.

> Now the glory of the LORD rested on Mount Sinai, and the cloud covered it six days. And on the seventh day He called to Moses out of the midst of the cloud. The sight of the glory of the LORD was like a consuming fire on the top of the mountain in the eyes of the children of Israel. (Exodus 24:16-17)

> And Moses and Aaron went into the tabernacle of meeting, and came out and blessed the people. Then the glory of the LORD appeared to all the people, and fire came out from before the LORD and consumed the burnt offering and the

fat on the altar. When all the people saw it, they shouted
and fell on their faces. (Leviticus 9:23-24)

When Solomon had finished praying, fire came down from
heaven and consumed the burnt offering and the sacrifices;
and the glory of the LORD filled the temple. (2 Chronicles 7:1)

The New International Version study notes state: "This manifestation
of God must have been staggering in its sudden and intense display of
his majesty and wrath." The glory of the Lord was enough to stop the
people from stoning the faithful spies, thus saving their lives.

God was displeased at the lack of faith shown by His people. All the
Israelites who were 20 years old and older would be punished by wandering one year in the wilderness for every day that the spies were in the
land; the journey that should have lasted a few months would now last 40
years as a result of their disobedience. For Caleb and Joshua, however,
their faith and trust would be rewarded. Not only would they enter the
Promised Land, but their lives would also be spared once again when
the other spies "died by the plague before the LORD" (Numbers 14:37).

Now the calendar jumps ahead about 40 years. Their 40 years of exile
were almost over, and the time fast approached for the Israelites to conquer
the Promised Land. Before they entered the land, the Lord described to
Moses the borders of their new home and the method by which the land
was to be allocated to each tribe. God also listed the men He had chosen to
oversee this process. We are not surprised to see the first name on the list of
leaders of the tribes is Caleb. Caleb is still trustworthy and faithful to God.

God's people then were able to end their 40 years in the wilderness.
For approximately five years they had been slowly taking control of
Canaan. It was time for Caleb, at age 85, to claim the land promised
to him so many years earlier. He approached Joshua, now the leader
in Moses' place, and asked for the mountain he had waited so long to
possess (Joshua 14:6-12). Joshua blessed Caleb and gave Hebron to him
as his inheritance in this new land. Unfortunately for Caleb, because
the people living there did not recognize Caleb as the new owner, he
had to fight for the land. These sons of Anak are the ones considered
"giants" although we might just think of them as "huge" or "gigantic."
The *Bible Background Commentary* tells us that one Egyptian letter describes

fierce warriors in Canaan that are 7 to 9 feet tall.[4] These were the ancestors of the famous Goliath. *Willmington's Bible Handbook* notes that the single tribe of Judah defeated these giants that had earlier scared off the entire nation of Israel.[5] Caleb did not lose heart as he defeated these fierce inhabitants and took the land as his own.

Othniel, Caleb's younger brother, captured the city of Kiriath Sepher for Caleb and, by virtue of the victory, was given Caleb's daughter Achsah as a wife. For a dowry, Caleb generously granted them the land of the Negev as well as springs of water. Othniel turned out to have his own place in the history of the Israelites. Judges 3:9 tells us that Othniel was raised up by God to become the first judge of Israel. Among Caleb's other not-so-illustrious descendants, we find the evil Nabal, husband of Abigail (1 Samuel 25:3). We are not told of Caleb's death or place of burial.

What Lessons Do We Learn From Caleb?

1. Caleb stood firm against the majority opinion.

The opinion of the majority is not always right. The majority of the spies recommended against advancing toward Canaan even though that was in opposition to God's plan. The majority of the Israelites cowered in fear and refused to obey God.

Our world today is frightening. CBS News conducted a poll in March 2013 in which 53 percent of Americans think it should be legal for same-sex couples to marry.[6] Does that make it right? Of course not. A Gallup poll in May 2013 asked if abortions should be legal under any circumstances, legal only under certain circumstances or illegal in all circumstances. A whopping 78 percent thought abortion should be legal under any circumstances or only under certain circumstances.[7] Does that make abortion right? No. As Christians, it is our responsibility to stand with God whether that counts us as part of the majority or not.

2. Caleb did not take the easy way out.

How much easier it would have been for Caleb and Joshua just to go along with the crowd. They could have stayed quiet and not opposed the other spies; they could have kept their mouths shut and avoided all kinds of trouble. Instead, they chose to take the hard path of righteousness.

If we take the easy way out in marriage, we might divorce when the first sign of trouble comes. The easy way out may be to stay quiet instead of confronting someone we love who is sinning. It might be easier to miss worship instead of making our plans around service times. Caleb did not take the easy way out of this situation, and neither should we.

3. Caleb suffered for doing the right thing.

Caleb tried to prevent the Israelites from disobeying God, but when he was unsuccessful, he was still kept out of Canaan along with the rest of the people. He had to endure not only the 40 years of wandering in the wilderness but also seeing his friends and family die one by one during that time.

Have you ever suffered for doing the right thing? I know one man who lost his job because he refused to go out drinking with his boss. Perhaps you lost a friend because her idea of fun was not compatible with your beliefs. Maybe you were humiliated by others when you dared to speak out against homosexuality or abortion. Noah, Joseph, Peter, Paul and many others suffered for doing what was right. Even though we might endure suffering in this life as Caleb did, we still need to strive to always do what is right.

4. God was pleased when Caleb fully followed Him.

Caleb was not wishy-washy in his obedience; he was not half-hearted in his declaration of faith in God but followed God completely.

> But My servant Caleb, because he has a different spirit in him and has followed Me fully, I will bring into the land where he went, and his descendants shall inherit it. (Numbers 14:24)

> Surely none of the men who came up from Egypt, from twenty years old and above, shall see the land of which I swore to Abraham, Isaac, and Jacob, because they have not wholly followed Me, except Caleb the son of Jephunneh, the Kenizzite, and Joshua the son of Nun, for they have wholly followed the LORD. (Numbers 32:11-12)

We know what it means when an athlete "goes all out" to win a ballgame or when someone "pulls out all the stops" to be successful. Caleb was just as determined that his words and actions would demonstrate his complete faith in God so that, like Paul, he could say, "I have fought the good fight, I have finished the race, I have kept the faith" (2 Timothy 4:7). David also reminds us of his submission to God in Psalm 119:10 when he writes, "With my whole heart I have sought You; oh, let me not wander from Your commandments!"

5. Caleb inherited the land he was promised.

God fulfilled His promise by giving Hebron to Caleb as his inheritance. Much like Caleb, we have been promised an inheritance as well.

And for this reason He is the Mediator of the new covenant, by means of death, for the redemption of the transgressions under the first covenant, that those who are called may receive the promise of the eternal inheritance. (Hebrews 9:15)

Blessed be the God and Father of our Lord Jesus Christ, who according to His abundant mercy has begotten us again to a living hope through the resurrection of Jesus Christ from the dead, to an inheritance incorruptible and undefiled and that does not fade away, reserved in heaven for you. (1 Peter 1:3-4)

Just as Caleb received his earthly inheritance, if we follow God fully, we will receive the heavenly inheritance that God has promised.

Caleb, as a spy, is not as famous as the modern spy James Bond, but as a servant of God, Caleb excelled. Proverbs 27:19 reminds us that as in water a face is reflected so the heart of man reveals the man. We can see the true heart of Caleb reflected in his actions. If we follow the example of faith and courage that he set for us long ago, like Caleb we will be pleasing to God Almighty.

Let's Think About This

1. Name some circumstances where the majority of people have gotten their way even though it was not right by God's standards.

2. Why do we sometimes choose the easy way instead of God's way?

3. Give examples of how Christians suffer for doing the right thing in today's world.

4. What does following God with all of your heart mean to you?

KORAH:
Mutiny on the Desert
Numbers 16:1-40; 26:9-11

T he idyllic life and beautiful women on the island of Tahiti proved to be too much temptation to the sailors. They wanted to stay on the lush island instead of continuing their voyage on the British Royal Navy ship, the *HMS Bounty*. On April 28, 1789, Fletcher Christian and his fellow mutineers set afloat their captain, Lieutenant William Bligh, along with some of his loyal crew in a small boat and then burned the *Bounty*. After 47 days, Bligh somehow managed to land in the Dutch East Indies and subsequently made his way back to Britain. The actions of Bligh and Christian became the basis for the 1932 novel *Mutiny on the Bounty* by Charles Nordhoff and James Norman Hall. In 1935 the film version starring Charles Laughton and Clark Gable became one of the biggest hits of its time.[1] Unfortunately, rebelling against leaders started long before 1789.

It is surprising how little we are told about what took place during the 40 years the Israelites wandered in the wilderness. One of the few incidents recorded for us, although we are not told exactly when this occurred during their journey, concerns a relative of Moses, a man named Korah. His story begins in Numbers 16 where we are told Korah is the son of Izhar (v. 1).

According to Exodus 6:18, Izhar was the brother of Amram, father of Aaron and Moses, making Korah a first cousin to Moses, leader of the Israelites. Of course Korah would also have been first cousin to Aaron, the high priest of the nation. Korah is a descendant of Levi so he would have been among those Levites who were named as guardians of the tabernacle whose duty it was to transport the tent and furnishings from place to place. Instead of offering sacrifices, his job would have been to carry furniture. The Levites were also assigned as assistants to the priests who were from the family of Aaron. Bear in mind that this type of priesthood was relatively new to the Israelites. Previously the heads of each family were the priests, and the priesthood was passed down to the eldest son. On Mount Sinai, after the exodus from Egypt, God established this priesthood with Aaron as the high priest and his sons as priests under him. Korah's point of view seemed to be that he could perform the duties of a priest just as well as his cousin Aaron. He was unhappy with what he perceived as his inferior role as an assistant to his relatives.

Korah teamed up with three men from the tribe of Reuben – Dathan, Abiram and On – who evidently had their own problems with the leadership in Israel. Reuben was the firstborn of all the Israelite tribes but had forfeited his right to primogeniture (Genesis 49:3-4). That big word means "Preference in inheritance that is given by law or custom to the eldest son and his issue." [2] Korah was not happy with his family's status among the Israelites and apparently neither were these Reubenites.

Miriam and Aaron previously had problems with their positions among the people and had spoken out against Moses as well, resulting in the Lord's striking Miriam with leprosy (Numbers 12:1-10). Korah and his cohorts must not have been paying attention, for they also decided to rebel against Moses. Are you curious how this all started? I wonder if Korah, Dathan, Abiram and On were sitting around the tent one night when one of them said, "I don't understand why Moses has so much authority. He is no better than the rest of us." One of the others might have answered, "That's the truth. I could get us out of this desert if I were in charge." Whatever the circumstances, they plotted to overthrow Moses and Aaron and convinced others to join them.

Korah and the others must have been men of influence because they were able to convince 250 princes or leaders of other tribes to unite in this conspiracy (Numbers 16:2). They called a meeting and openly challenged the authority of Moses and Aaron. The reason publicly stated for their complaint centered on the fact that all of them were holy, not just Moses and Aaron (Exodus 19:6). Those in rebellion argued that because God had made them "a kingdom of priests" Moses and Aaron should not be in positions of leadership. It seems Korah kept mum in the beginning about his desire for the priesthood which was his underlying reason for the mutiny.

Upon hearing their complaints, Moses fell on his face, probably bowing in prayer (Numbers 16:4). Moses did not argue with Korah; he did not take up for himself; he did not call for the people to fight against these men. Instead, he left it up to God. Moses proposed a test to settle the dispute. They were all to bring censers the next day to offer incense to the Lord. The censers were containers shaped somewhat like a bowl with a handle.[3] *Easton's Bible Dictionary* explains that normally the priest filled the censer with live coals from the fire on the altar of burnt-offering, carried it into the sanctuary, and then threw the sweet incense upon the burning coals sending up a cloud of smoke and filling the air with fragrance (Leviticus 16:12-13).[4] The censers of the 250 men were probably ones that had been used to offer incense to household deities by the Egyptians. When the Israelites left Egypt, the censers were most likely among the articles of gold and silver given to them by their Egyptian neighbors (Exodus 12:35).[5] The attitude of Moses seemed to be that, if Korah and his friends thought they could act like priests, let them bring incense to offer and then they would see whose offering God accepted.

I love how Moses echoes the words of this mutinous group when he says in Numbers 16:7, "You take too much upon yourselves, you sons of Levi!" The New Century Version reads, "You Levites have gone too far." In other words, it is not I; it is you who have transgressed.

Moses emphasized that the Levites had already been chosen for a special ministry to God in their service in the tabernacle. Wasn't that enough? Moses questioned why they were also now seeking the priesthood itself. And why attack Aaron? Aaron had done nothing against these men, and yet he was a focus of their grumbling. The priesthood of Aaron came directly from God; by refusing it, these men were rejecting

God.[6] We can almost see Moses shaking his head at the absurdity of their actions.

Moses wanted to talk directly to Dathan and Abiram. Notice that On is no longer mentioned in the narrative. It is possible that he withdrew from the revolt although we are not told the reason for his absence. Dathan and Abiram refused to comply with the summons. The *Jamieson, Fausset, and Brown Commentary* tells us: "The phrase, 'We will not come up!' (Numbers 16:12, 14), is used here not in a geographical or physical, but a moral sense, according to a Hebrew idiom, to denote an appearance before a judge or king." [7] Perhaps Moses wanted them to come to the front of the crowd so he could see their faces when he spoke to them, but they would not consent to face him. Their words, however, were directed to Moses when they accused him of bringing them to die in the wilderness instead of staying in Egypt, what they called "the land flowing with milk and honey" (v. 14), a phrase that had earlier described the Promised Land. What a slap in the face! Moses had challenged Pharaoh for these people; he had risked his life along with theirs when they faced the Egyptian army; he had suffered hunger and thirst by their sides during their journey. Now he was confronted with allegations that he wanted to exert his power over them.

Moses was fed up with their charges and asserted his innocence. He had never done anything wrong to these men; he had not so much as taken a donkey from any of them (Numbers 16:15). Moses implored God not to accept the offerings from these rebellious men.

> So every man took his censer, put fire in it, laid incense on it, and stood at the door of the tabernacle of meeting with Moses and Aaron. And Korah gathered all the congregation against them at the door of the tabernacle of meeting. Then the glory of the LORD appeared to all the congregation. (Numbers 16:18-19)

These men really wanted to act like priests, didn't they? They all gathered at the doorway of the tabernacle with their censers and burning coals and incense. Korah apparently wanted witnesses so he assembled the Israelites to watch what would happen. "Then the glory of the LORD appeared to all the congregation" (Numbers 16:19). The glory of the Lord usually appeared as a bright shining light to signify God's presence among the people.

God was so angry at the scene before Him that He was going to destroy all the people. Once again, we see the reverence of Moses and Aaron as they fell on their faces before the Lord. Moses intervened on the Israelites' behalf, begging God not to be angry with them all because of the sins of one (Numbers 16:22).

The logistics of what happened next are a little hard for us to follow. It seems that Dathan and Abiram were near their tents while Korah and his men had gone to the tabernacle. Spectators were probably everywhere, watching to see what would happen before they were told to separate themselves from those directly involved. Dathan and Abiram and their families stood defiantly in the doorways of their tents.

> Now it came to pass, as he finished speaking all these words, that the ground split apart under them, and the earth opened its mouth and swallowed them up, with their households and all the men with Korah, with all their goods. So they and all those with them went down alive into the pit; the earth closed over them, and they perished from among the assembly. (Numbers 16:31-33)

Can you imagine the horror of this scene? Can you hear the screams? As the Israelites watched, the ground opened up, swallowing the families of Dathan and Abiram and all their possessions – even their tents. No physical evidence of their existence remained; they were wiped off the face of the earth. This was no chance occurrence, no coincidence; rather, it was the almighty God punishing sinners. The people panicked at the sight and ran away, afraid that they, too, might be devoured.

The 250 men offering incense at the tabernacle suffered a different fate. Numbers 16:35 reports that fire came out from the Lord and consumed them. It seems ironic that they were trying to present themselves before the Lord as priests with fire, and it was fire that claimed their lives. We are not really told what happened to Korah in all this, whether he died in the earthquake or the fire. Psalm 106:16-18 specifies Dathan and Abiram being swallowed up which makes us think Korah probably stood with the 250 men offering incense and died by fire. Jude mentions "the rebellion of Korah" that led to perishing (v. 11).

What Lessons Do We Learn From Korah and His Co-conspirators?

1. It is easy to get swept up in sin.

Korah seemed to be the ringleader of the group challenging the authority of Moses and Aaron, but then Dathan, Abiram and On got involved, later to be joined by 250 leaders of the congregation. When everyone around us is complaining or grumbling, it is easy to be persuaded to chip in our two cents worth. When others are participating in sin in our presence, it is simple just to go along. We get caught up in the moment and before we know it, we have said or done things that we should not. Would Dathan or Abiram or those 250 men have ever openly opposed Moses if not for the evil influence of Korah? We will never know the answer.

2. We should not oppose God's ways.

Korah had lost this battle before it ever started because God is always going to win. We are reminded in Proverbs 21:30, "There is no wisdom or understanding or counsel against the LORD." We will never outsmart God; we will never be able to come up with better strategies or superior plans than God, and we must not even try.

For My thoughts are not your thoughts, nor are your ways My ways," says the LORD. For as the heavens are higher than the earth, so are My ways higher than your ways, and My thoughts than your thoughts. (Isaiah 55:8-9)

In Acts 11:17, when Peter was delivering his argument for preaching the gospel to the Gentiles, he stated, "If therefore God gave them the same gift as He gave us when we believed on the Lord Jesus Christ, who was I that I could withstand God?" If God desired that His grace be extended to the Gentiles, who could deny Him that privilege? Faithful Christians should always be willing to surrender their wills to the will of God.

3. We are to submit to authority.

Korah would not recognize the authority of Moses and Aaron given to them by God, and he did not want to submit to them. The selfish desire for greatness and authority is a common theme in Scripture whether it's Korah opposing Moses and Aaron, Absalom defying his father (2 Samuel 15), Adonijah claiming the crown (1 Kings 1), the disciples arguing over which of them was the greatest (Luke 22:24), or Diotrephes loving to have preeminence in the local church (3 John 9-10). We are admonished in Hebrews 13:17: "Obey those who rule over you, and be submissive, for they watch out for your souls, as those who must give account. Let them do so with joy and not with grief, for that would be unprofitable for you." Someone has to be in charge. God clearly wants us to be obedient to the leaders He has placed before us.

4. Pride can have disastrous results.

David addresses the problem of pride in Psalm 31:18 when he writes: "Let the lying lips be put to silence, which speak insolent things proudly and contemptuously against the righteous." Pride is identified as evil in Proverbs 8:13: "The fear of the LORD is to hate evil; Pride and arrogance and the evil way and the perverse mouth I hate."

Don't these verses sound exactly like Korah as well as Dathan and Abiram? Pride and arrogance go hand in hand, and we see them both in Korah when he thought he should be part of the priesthood. We can imagine Korah thinking, "Why should Aaron be exalted above me? Who does Aaron think he is anyway? I am just as good as those priests." We are familiar with Proverbs 16:18 that reads, "Pride goes before destruction, and a haughty spirit before a fall." This wise saying certainly applied to these men. How much better off they would have been if they had lived by the words of Paul that would be written to the Ephesians:

Let all bitterness, wrath, anger, clamor, and evil speaking be put away from you, with all malice. And be kind to one another, tenderhearted, forgiving one another, even as God in Christ forgave you. (Ephesians 4:31-32)

5. We should separate ourselves from sinners.

Moses told those in the congregation to separate themselves from these wicked men and not even to touch anything that belonged to them. A wonderful Bible School teacher once passed around to her class a block of wood that had been covered with carbon paper. As the children each touched it, their fingers became blackened. She pointed out that sin was the same way. We can't come in contact with sin without becoming dirty ourselves. The wise writer of Proverbs continually admonishes us to steer clear of those who are evil so as to keep ourselves clean from sin. "Do not enter the path of the wicked, and do not walk in the way of evil. Avoid it, do not travel on it; turn away from it and pass on" (Proverbs 4:14-15).

Korah, Dathan, Abiram and 250 leaders of the Israelites allowed the sin of pride to lead to their destruction. Instead of humbling themselves before God, they strove to elevate themselves and paid for it with their lives. We need to erase pride and haughtiness from our lives in order to be pleasing to our God.

Let's Think About This

1. How would you describe Korah's character?

2. Do a Bible search to find other times that "the glory of the Lord" appeared.

3. How does Proverbs 21:24 relate to Korah?

4. In what ways do people today act as if their ways are better than God's way?

5. Who else in Scripture desired authority he or she did not deserve?

Exod 19:6
Num 12:3
    " 26:11
1 Cor 15:33
Jude 1:11
Matt 7:15   **46**
Acts 20:29-30

ACHAN:
Caught Red-Handed

Joshua 6:18-24; 7:1-26

The picture that was in the newspaper in 1967 is buried away with my other keepsakes. I was a member of the forensics club in high school and participated in speech tournaments around the Tennessee and Kentucky area, even flying to Washington, D.C., twice to represent our school in a tournament. My areas of competition included debating and extemporaneous speaking. In the National Forensic League, we received points based on how well we did. If we won our division, we received so many points; if we came in second, we were granted fewer points and so on. At the end of the school year, we attended a big banquet and awards were given out for the students with the highest points for the year.

I knew how many points I had obtained and that I had a chance of winning the top award for girls that year, but one girl from another school might have beaten me because I did not know how many points she had accumulated. It was so nerve-racking waiting as the names were called ever so slowly. With only the top two places to announce, she and I were both nervously waiting. The emcee for the evening finally was ready to call the name of the second-place winner. He announced her name. I had won! I remember the joy of winning, but I also remember the agony of waiting while the names were called. One particular man from the book of Joshua could probably identify with my nervous feelings.

Unsung Heroes (and a Few Villains)

The Israelites were on the verge of entering the Promised Land where lush fields, good soil and a new life were waiting to be theirs. To take over the land, however, they had to conquer the Canaanites in each city, beginning with the battle for the city of Jericho. The Lord encouraged Joshua by His announcement that He was giving Jericho into their hands. The Israelites were to march silently around the city walls one time each day for six days. On the seventh day they were to circle the city seven times. The priests would blow their trumpets, and the people would shout with a great shout, and the walls would collapse, allowing the people to go in and destroy the city. Only Rahab, the woman who had earlier protected the Israelite spies, would be saved along with her family. God gave them one other charge. Everything in the city would be "doomed by the LORD to destruction" (Joshua 6:17) with the exception of silver, gold, bronze and iron which would be "consecrated to the LORD" (v. 19).

Everything happened just as the Lord said it would. The walls of Jericho came tumbling down, and the Israelites overtook the city. Rahab and her family were protected and then the city was burned. Joshua 6:24 tells us that the silver and gold as well as articles of bronze and iron were put into the treasury of the Lord's house. But not all of the silver and gold wound up where it was supposed to. In Joshua 7:1 we are introduced to Achan from the tribe of Judah. His name means "one who troubles,"[1] and he certainly troubled Israel when he took some items doomed to destruction, and God was angry. Even though Achan was just one man, Israel was seen as one entity, and as a result, when one sinned, the responsibility was shared by the whole group. Thus, God's anger extended to the whole nation.[2]

Jericho was the first city to be conquered in this new land. Because all went well, Joshua turned his attention to the smaller town of Ai. Spies were sent in to determine how best to proceed against Ai. Because it was just a small town with probably around 12,000 inhabitants,[3] Joshua's spies recommended that only about 3,000 soldiers needed to go in to overtake it. When the Israelites attacked, however, things did not go as planned. Ai decisively defeated the Israelites, resulting in the deaths of 36 soldiers. Such an unexpected loss completely deflated the confidence of the Israelites. Where was God? Why had He not helped them defeat Ai as He did Jericho? What had gone wrong?

Joshua tore his clothes to show his distress; he and the elders of Israel put dust on their heads as they mourned this great loss. They recognized that for some unknown reason the Lord had not been with them in battle. Without God on their side, their mission of conquering the entire land would be impossible. The other Canaanites would hear of this downfall and be even stronger in their resistance. Joshua prayed to God, insinuating that the loss was somehow God's fault and even implying that maybe the Israelites would have been better off just to have stayed out of the Promised Land.

> "And Joshua said, "Alas, Lord GOD, why have You brought this people over the Jordan at all – to deliver us into the hand of the Amorites, to destroy us? Oh, that we had been content, and dwelt on the other side of the Jordan!" (Joshua 7:7).

God in His mercy answered Joshua's prayer, explaining that this defeat, Israel's first and only military defeat in Canaan,[4] was a direct result of Israel's sin. Someone had taken some things that belonged to God. Note the end of Joshua 7:11: "and they have also put it among their own stuff." God said that someone had taken some of the things from Ai and acted as if those things belonged to the thief instead of God. God refused to be with them anymore until this matter was settled.

Certain steps needed to be taken in order to rid the nation of this evil. The people needed to be cleansed to be ritually pure for the next day when they would come before the Lord. This included washing in addition to avoiding contact with those things that would make them unclean.[5] God would point out the guilty party by process of elimination. First, the tribes would come forth, then the families, then the households, and finally the man who was guilty of this gross sin would be identified. Some of the versions say this was done "by lot." According to *Barnes' Notes*, the Hebrew word for lot suggests that small stones, probably white and black ones, were used for this process.[6] The stones were most likely drawn from a chest to show the answer to questions asked, such as, "Is the guilty party from this family?" We are reminded of the Urim and Thummin used to determine God's will in certain instances (Numbers 27:21; Ezra 2:63), although no one knows precisely how they worked either.

Unsung Heroes (and a Few Villains)

All the people came before Joshua by tribes. The tribe of Judah was chosen; the family of the Zarhites was chosen; the household of Zabdi was chosen. I am not sure we can begin to imagine the anxiety and dread of Achan as this was taking place. Have you ever been in a situation where you were waiting to see if your name was called? Maybe names were being drawn from a pool for jury duty; perhaps you were in a competition as I was and they were announcing the winners. You nervously waited each time another name was called out. Think about Achan. He knew his name was going to come up in the end, but he had to sit through the entire process as Joshua slowly progressed closer and closer to naming Achan as the perpetrator who brought defeat to the whole nation. His fate was sealed, and he knew it just as he knew it was wrong to take those things which belonged to the Lord. Finally the excruciating wait was over. Achan was designated as the sinner responsible for this crushing blow to the Israelites.

Joshua admonished Achan to confess what he had done. Achan didn't seem to have much choice at that point; thankfully he admitted his sin. Achan acknowledged that he had stolen a beautiful robe, gold and silver. Some versions call this robe a "Babylonian garment" because Babylon was built on the plain of Shinar. This would have been a costly garment, probably a long robe such as was worn by kings and could possibly have belonged to the king of Jericho.[7] These robes were often beautifully dyed and richly embroidered. The 200 shekels of silver would weigh approximately 5 to 6 pounds, and the gold would be about 1.5 pounds. It would have taken the average person a lifetime to earn these riches.[8] Achan even revealed how it happened. He saw the objects, coveted them, took the items and hid them in his tent. We are reminded of Eve who followed this same progression of sin. She saw the fruit, coveted it, took it and then tried to hide her sin. King David is another example of this pattern in his dealings with Bathsheba. He saw her, desired her, took her and then went to great lengths to hide what he had done.

Messengers ran to the tent and, sure enough, the stolen property was hidden underneath the dirt floor of the tent. Joshua had to act to erase this sin from the camp. Joshua took Achan, the stolen items, Achan's animals, his tent and his family and brought them to the Valley of Achor where he pronounced Achan's punishment.

Achan had been found guilty, and his sentence was declared to be death by stoning. Stoning is the most commonly mentioned form of capital punishment in the Scriptures. It is a punishment delivered by the whole community because the sin was against the whole community.[9] Depending on the version you read, these verses sound as if the whole family may have been stoned to death. The question has been raised, "Did his family really die along with him, and if so, why?" Deuteronomy 24:16 prohibited children from being put to death for the sins of their father. It is possible Achan's family was brought to the valley with Achan just to witness the execution. Most Bible commentators, however, conclude that the family was included in the death sentence, probably because they were somehow complicit in his crime. It is certainly plausible that they were aware of the items buried under their home, and they kept quiet instead of exposing their father, turning them into accomplices of his crime. Stoning the entire family would have the effect of obliterating the family line. By burning the bodies afterward with fire, the land was purged from this evil.

What Lessons Do We Learn From Achan?

1. Never underestimate the amount of damage one person's sin can cause.

The whole Israelite nation suffered as a result of Achan's sin. "Did not Achan the son of Zerah commit a trespass in the accursed thing, and wrath fell on all the congregation of Israel? And that man did not perish alone in his iniquity" (Joshua 22:20).

When the Israelites attacked Ai, 36 soldiers lost their lives in the battle because God had deserted them as a direct result of Achan's sin. Those men and their families certainly suffered because of his actions. The nation of Israel endured discouragement and doubt due to his theft. Those closest to him, his family, also suffered, for we assume they lost their lives in the stoning.

It is easy to look at a drug addict and point out the damage done to his family and friends. Children may suffer when their parents commit crimes and wind up in prison. But we needn't go to such extremes to see the suffering caused to innocent victims of sins. Children suffer when parents argue. Families are often torn apart when a spouse has an extramarital affair. Gossiping can ruin reputations. Sins affect people other than just the sinner.

2. Sin is never hidden from God.

Achan thought he could hide his sin by burying the stolen objects, but God wasn't fooled. "The eyes of the LORD are in every place, keeping watch on the evil and the good" (Proverbs 15:3).

We are reminded of the song that contains these words, "There's an all-seeing Eye watching you." God is watching, and we must be aware that we will never be successful in trying to hide our sin from Him. Numbers 32:23 specifically says, "Be sure your sin will find you out."

3. We must not linger near those things that are forbidden.

As Barney Fife used to say, we need to "Nip it! Nip it in the bud!" We need to stop sin before it starts. Remember that progression of Achan's sin? He saw the valuable objects, coveted them, took them and hid them in his tent. How much better off he would have been to have left them where he found them. James tells us, "But each one is tempted when he is drawn away by his own desires and enticed. Then, when desire has conceived, it gives birth to sin; and sin, when it is full-grown, brings forth death" (1:14-15).

If Achan had never let the thought of having those riches linger in his mind but instead had immediately "run for the hills" as Joseph did when confronted with temptation, the whole history of the Israelite nation could have been different. The Israelite army would not have been defeated at Ai; those 36 soldiers would not have lost their lives; Achan would not have been punished for his sin.

Do we linger near things that are forbidden? Maybe we spend too much time longing over possessions we cannot really afford. A man might take a second glance at a woman that leads to sin. Perhaps we read books or watch movies we know are exposing us to sin. Do you know people who go to casinos to gamble "just a little" and then are swallowed up by the temptation of riches? When we see those things that are an enticement to sin, we must have the strength and wisdom to withdraw ourselves before we are plunged into the downward progression of sin.

4. We must not rob God.

During this first conquest in Canaan, certain items were to be given to God for His glory, for only through Him was victory possible, but Achan chose to steal from God, to take those things which properly belonged to Jehovah.

> *Will a man rob God? Yet you have robbed Me! But you say,*
> *"In what way have we robbed You?" In tithes and offerings.*
> *You are cursed with a curse, for you have robbed Me,*
> *even this whole nation. (Malachi 3:8-9)*

What do we steal from God? Do we hold back our riches that could be used for His glory and honor? Is our time kept back from His purposes? Do we rob Him of honor when we take credit for the talents He has given us? If we honor God as our Lord and Master, we will joyfully give Him all that is due Him.

Achan found out the hard way that the riches of this world are not worth disobedience to God. A heap of stones was placed over his burnt remains as a symbol and reminder of his shameful act so that as people passed by and heard the story of Achan, they would be reminded of his detestable crime (Joshua 7:26). As Christians, we also need to remember his wicked example.

Let's Think About This

1. Name other examples in Scripture where harm was caused by the sin of one person.

2. How do others suffer because of the sins we commit?

3. How do we try to hide our sins from God?

4. How can we thwart temptation before it is too late?

5. What do we steal from God?

BOAZ:
A True Gentleman

Ruth 1–4

have a copy of a letter written by my grandfather, Forrest Poole, to my grandmother, Lelan, when they were dating in 1918. This excerpt from the letter lets us take a glimpse into the past.

Adams, Tenn., Jan. 3, 1918

Received your letter last night; was glad to hear from you again. Had almost began to think that you was never going to write anymore. Say, listen, Lelan dear. I am going to say something that I don't want to write, but owing to something, I am going to write it anyway. Say dear, I do not know how to say what I am about to say except that I love you and want you to be my wife. Probably you will think that I should have asked you the last time I saw you, but then I had not decided that I should and not knowing just when I could see you again and as I must or at least want to know by next Sunday or Monday, I thought it best to write to you today. Listen dear, you know that I love you and have loved you for some time, but I tell you honestly and truly I have loved you ever since I saw you the first time. It is true that I did not go with you for one whole summer, but nevertheless, I loved you just the same for I never hardly went with another girl all that summer for thinking about you. Listen dear I haven't much to offer you except my heart and health, but if you will accept these I will promise you truly that if you will accept these that I will always love and cherish you. Listen dear, please don't say no if you only have a little love for me because you don't know what this means to me. Say, listen Lelan dear, think over what I have said and then give me your answer whatever it may be. If you find it in your heart to say yes, it will make me the proudest man in the whole U.S.A. But if you don't, no one will say or know that you said no to me. Well, dear, I must close and carry this to the mailbox as Mr. Edwards is almost due. Say, Lelan, won't you please say yes if you possibly can and remember that if you do, I will be the happiest man that you ever heard of. Say dear, if you cannot say yes, will you promise me to burn this up and not say a word about this letter? Well, I must close this letter. Hoping to hear from you soon.

Truly and sincerely, Forrest

Isn't that sweet? Of course, she said yes, and they were happily married for more than 50 years.

An earlier love story began during a time of tragedy when Israel was facing a famine. In the small town of Bethlehem lived a man by the name of Elimelech along with his family; however, feeding his wife Naomi and two sons had become difficult during the famine. Elimelech decided to take his family to the land of Moab, a journey of 70 to 100 miles depending on which route they took. It would have taken approximately a week to travel this distance.[1] Misfortune followed when, after a time, Elimelech died. The two sons married Moabite women, but after 10 years, both sons also died. What heartbreak for Naomi. She lost not only her husband but also her sons. The situation was very bleak as women lost all social status and economic security when their husbands died, and they had to depend on society for their well-being. Widows would have been the equivalent of the homeless in our culture today.[2]

Upon hearing that food was available in the land of Judah, Naomi decided to return to her homeland. She encouraged her daughters-in-law to go back to their families where they could remarry and start a new life. Her daughter-in-law Orpah said a tearful goodbye and left, but Ruth, her remaining daughter-in-law, refused to leave and instead promised to stay with Naomi. Naomi and Ruth traveled to Bethlehem, arriving just at the beginning of the barley harvest which would have been about mid-to-late April.[3]

Naomi and Ruth still had a big problem because they had no means of support and needed food to eat. Per God's instructions, Moses had directed the property owners to intentionally leave some grain in the fields for "the poor and the stranger" to gather (Leviticus 19:9-10). Ruth volunteered to go and find such a field and "glean," meaning to pick up whatever grain was dropped (Ruth 2:2).

Boaz, a relative of Naomi's dead husband, Elimelech, entered the picture. Boaz, a wealthy Bethlehemite, was the son of Salmon and his wife Rahab (Matthew 1:5), whom we know as the harlot who earlier had hidden the two Israelite spies. Boaz saw the young woman following his reapers in the field and inquired about her. He kindly spoke to Ruth and encouraged her to continue to work in his fields, even offering protection to her and water to drink. Ruth bowed before him and asked, "Why have I found favor in your eyes, that you should take notice of me, since I am a foreigner?" (Ruth 2:10). Boaz explained that Ruth's reputation had preceded her; he had heard about all she had done for Naomi and the hardships they had suffered. The kind Boaz arranged for her to eat alongside his workers and even went so far as to instruct his servants purposefully to leave some grain for her so that her job would be easier. When Ruth went home to Naomi and told her what had happened, Naomi realized that this was good because Boaz was a close relative who would protect Ruth. Ruth continually returned to the fields of Boaz until the end of both the barley harvest and the wheat harvest which would have taken several weeks.

Naomi thought about the situation and came up with an idea to provide for their long-term security. She instructed Ruth to wash herself and put on her best clothes. Water was not always plentiful in this part of the world and frequent bathing was not common. In effect Naomi was really telling Ruth to put off the garments of a widow and prepare as a bride for her wedding.[4] Ruth was to go to the threshing floor where Boaz was having an end-of-the-harvest feast but to be careful not to let herself be seen until he had finished eating. This reminds me of my grandfather's letter when he wrote not to let anybody know about the proposal if she said no. Naomi did not want others to know what was going on in case the plan did not work out. Ruth did exactly as Naomi instructed. At the threshing floor, men placed the sheaves on the floor and then separated the grain from the stalks by either having oxen walk on it or by beating the stalks. When the grain was separated, the workers would throw the grain into the air and the breeze would carry the chaff away while the grain fell to the floor to be gathered. This job would often be done in the evening when there was a good breeze and then each owner would sleep on the floor to protect his harvest.[5]

What happened next sounds very strange. Ruth quietly tiptoed in and lay down at the feet of Boaz or "uncovered his feet" (Ruth 3:7). We would say she reclined at the foot of the bed. Boaz probably slept on a mat or skin of some kind and Ruth positioned herself crosswise at his feet, a position in which Eastern servants frequently slept in the same chamber or tent as their master. Remember they would sleep in the same clothes they wore during the day so there was no impropriety there.[6]

At church camp, I once crawled in my sleeping bag only to discover a frog had been placed in the bottom of it. It didn't take me long to realize something was at my feet. About midnight Boaz felt something at his feet as well; as a result he "turned himself" (Ruth 3:8) or bent forward to find out what was there. Imagine his surprise when he found a woman. In the dark and being awakened from sleep, he did not recognize her. Ruth identified herself and asked him to "take your maidservant under your wing" (v. 9). In other words, she proposed to him. The New American Standard Bible reads, "Spread your covering over your maid." To spread one's cover over a person meant to claim that person for yourself.[7] In this instance, the phrase signified acknowledging her as his wife. Ruth was asking Boaz to obey the law of the kinsman redeemer. This kinsman would buy property from a poor relative in order to keep the land in the family. "If one of your brethren becomes poor, and has sold some of his possession, and if his redeeming relative comes to redeem it, then he may redeem what his brother sold" (Leviticus 25:25).

It was also the duty of the brother of a dead man to take the man's wife and have children with her for the dead brother in order to facilitate a line of inheritance, as we read in Deuteronomy 25:5-10. If there was no living brother, as in this case, the responsibility reverted to the closest male relative.

We need to consider the point of view of Boaz. Ruth was evidently a good bit younger than Boaz. She was so poor she had to depend on the welfare system of that day to supply even her most basic needs. She was a foreigner from the land of Moab. It would cost money to redeem her dead husband's land in order to marry her. None of this would make her a good prospect for a wife from his standpoint, yet Boaz accepted her proposal willingly. Before wedding plans could be made, though, there was a snag. Another relative even closer than Boaz had the first option on the land. Boaz quietly sent Ruth home without others knowing of her presence in order to prevent gossip and perhaps mar the integrity of the legal arrangement. The next morning Boaz went to the city gate where the court of justice was commonly held,[8] and it just so happened (Do we see God's hand at work here?) that the man who was a closer relative to Elimelech happened by. Boaz invited the man to join him as he gathered 10 of the city elders to serve as witnesses. Ten was probably the number needed to constitute a lawful public assembly.[9] Boaz explained the situation regarding Naomi and the land that belonged to Elimelech. At first, this relative said, "Sure, I will redeem it," but then came the fly in the ointment.

Boaz made it clear that if this man took the land, he also had to take Ruth whereupon the man immediately backed off. Perhaps he already had a wife and didn't want another; perhaps he was afraid it would adversely affect his financial situation. Whatever the reason, he declined. The custom at that time to confirm a transaction was for one man to remove his sandal which Elimelech's relative did in front of the 10 witnesses, turning over his rights to Boaz. Boaz won the land and the girl.

In due time, Boaz and Ruth's marriage was blessed with a son they named Obed who became the great-grandfather of David.

What Lessons Do We Learn From the Life of Boaz?

1. Boaz was honorable.

A good reputation was important to him. Boaz helped protect the reputation of Ruth by ordering his servants not to touch her. He also remarked that he had heard about her reputation, noting all she had done for her mother-in-law. When Ruth showed up at the foot of his bed, he made sure she left before word got out that she was there and caused people to talk.

A good name is to be chosen rather than great riches, loving favor rather than silver and gold. (Proverbs 22:1)

Pray for us; for we are confident that we have a good conscience, in all things desiring to live honorably. (Hebrews 13:18)

An honorable reputation should also be important to us as Christians. If people think of us as good, honest and faithful, it will be easier to reach them with the gospel. The opposite of that is also true. If my reputation is as someone who lies or cheats or acts hatefully, then people won't come to me to learn the truth about Jesus. The way others perceive our character should matter to us. We need to consider carefully how our actions and words will affect our reputations.

2. Boaz was kind and caring.

He spoke to his workers with kindness, "May the LORD be with you" (Ruth 2:4). He certainly was kind to Ruth, this poor foreign widow whom he took under his protection. Boaz also showed concern for Naomi by sending enough food for her to have plenty to eat.

And be kind to one another, tenderhearted, forgiving one another, even as God in Christ forgave you. (Ephesians 4:32)

Therefore, as we have opportunity, let us do good to all, especially to those who are of the household of faith. (Galatians 6:10)

The ancient Greek storyteller Aesop is quoted as having written, "No act of kindness, no matter how small, is ever wasted." [10] American author Samuel Clemens, better known by his pen name Mark Twain, wisely wrote, "Kindness is the language which the deaf can hear and the blind can see." [11] We should be like Jesus who repeatedly showed kindness as He blessed the children, taught the woman from Samaria, healed the lepers and provided food for the multitudes. Being kind to others should be more than a cliché; it should be a way of life for the Christian.

3. Boaz was a rule-follower.

Even though he knew he wanted to marry Ruth, Boaz went through the proper channels. He went to the city elders; he talked to the man who was a closer relative; he proceeded with the agreement legally. God wants rules followed and things done in the right order. God has proclaimed marriage before children, maturity before eldership, repentance and baptism before salvation. I am reminded of a young woman I know. She and her boyfriend lived together; then they married; then they had a bridal shower. I remember thinking, "Wait! That is backward." God wants us to be rule-followers as Boaz was, keeping things in the proper order.

He who heeds the word wisely will find good, and whoever trusts in the Lord, happy is he. (Proverbs 16:20)

Boaz was a good man; he was a faithful follower of God. He reached out to help someone in need and wound up being in the lineage of Jesus Christ (Matthew 1:5). What a wonderful example he left for us to follow.

Let's Think About This   *Isaiah 54:10*

1. Why do you think Ruth decided to stay with Naomi instead of going back to her family?   *Psalm 144:15*

2. Discuss the qualities of Boaz that made him a good employer.

3. Ruth was a poor, foreign widow, but Boaz did not let any of that stop him from marrying her. Why? Do you think his mother's lineage played a role in his decision?

4. Think of someone you know who is honorable. Describe the qualities that you admire in that person.   *"Kindness"*

Boaz was godly Ruth 2:4
open-minded, merciful v 11,12
generous v 14-16
[discreet Ruth 3:9-14
[respectful
faithful & dilligent Ruth 4:9-10
Matt 1:5 - Boaz's father & mother

NABAL'S SERVANT:
Standing Up and Speaking Out
1 Samuel 25:1-38

In Joshua, Texas, Remington Reimer worked hard to become the local high school valedictorian of 2013. In June, he stood before classmates, parents and friends at the graduation ceremony to make his valedictory speech. Everything was going fine until he deviated from his pre-approved comments and began to mention God and the Constitution; suddenly, everything went quiet. The audience could no longer hear his words because the school officials had turned off his microphone.[1]

Roy Costner IV was the 2013 valedictorian for the Liberty High School in Pickens County, S.C. When he was on stage to present his pre-approved speech, he instead ripped the paper in half, made a few off-the-cuff remarks, and then recited the Lord's Prayer in defiance of the school district's decision no longer to include prayer at graduation ceremonies. His actions drew loud applause and cheers from the audience. Atheist groups had complained about prayers in public school gatherings so the district officials had decided to end invocations at all school functions and replace prayer at high school graduations with a moment of silence. Costner decided he wasn't going to let activist groups kick God out of his graduation. "Our Father, who art in Heaven, hallowed be Thy name," Costner declared. "Thy Kingdom come … " The people in attendance realized that Costner was reciting the Lord's Prayer, and applause began to break out in the coliseum. Within seconds, the applause was accompanied by loud cheers.[2]

What courage these two young men demonstrated by their commitment to stand up for what was right. In Scripture, another young man made the same decision – to stand up and speak out for the truth.

King Saul was unwavering in his determination to kill David, the man slated to take over the throne of Israel. David and all the men who supported him were considered outlaws, traitors and fugitives. For a period of 17 years, David had to live as a fugitive, fleeing from Saul, frequently hiding in the wilderness of Judah. Sometime during one of those stays in the wilderness, David and his men happened upon a group of shepherds caring for their flocks. The shepherds must have been surprised when David and his men offered them protection and kindness instead of trouble.

Later David and his men happened to be near Carmel, a city in the district of Maon in Judah. King Saul had been in this town previously and had left a monument of himself behind (1 Samuel 15:12). Evidently people here were loyal fans of Saul. While in the area, David heard that a rich herder was shearing his sheep and having a great feast. It turned out this was the same flock of sheep David had helped protect previously. David sent a message by 10 of his men to the owner of the sheep politely asking that they share some provisions with him and his men. After all, hadn't they protected the owner's sheep from wild animals and raiders? Didn't they deserve something for that? Nabal sent back his reply, but it was not the one David was expecting.

Nabal arrogantly turned down the request. He not only refused, but he was downright ugly about it; he would not even send bread and water. In the process, he insulted David saying, "Who is this David? Why should I give my food to him?" Maybe he knew helping David would not benefit him in the king's eyes; giving food to the king's enemy might be a bad political move. *1 Sam 25:10*

When David's messengers told David what Nabal had said, he was angry. He had been kind to Nabal's men, and this was how he was treated in return. David was furious. He and 400 of his men grabbed their swords and headed out after Nabal. In the meantime, "back at the ranch," one of the servants told Nabal's wife, Abigail, what had happened. He told her how kind David had been, how hateful Nabal had been and how trouble was surely on its way.

In various Bible translations, this unnamed man (1 Samuel 25:14) is called a "servant" (NIV, ERV) or a young man (KJV, ESV, NKJV, NASB). David refers to the men he had previously given protection to as "shepherds" (v. 7). From his conversation with Abigail, we learn that this young servant had been one of the shepherds in the previous encounter with David (vv. 15-16). This young shepherd knew he did not have the authority himself to do anything to prevent this situation, but surely he could do something. He informed Abigail of what was happening. He told how her husband abruptly rejected David's request; then he proceeded to tell her about David. He had obviously been out in the fields with the sheep when they had encountered David and had direct interaction with David's band of men. He related what happened from personal experience, explaining how good David's men had been to the shepherds, how honest they were and how they even protected them day and night.

This servant took a lot of responsibility upon himself when he went to Abigail, his master's wife, and told her what was going on. You remember the story of Esther who knew she would die along with all the other Jews if she didn't take action (Esther 4:14). Maybe that is how this man felt. If David and his men came wielding swords, he knew none of them had a chance of survival, including himself. He may have been taking a chance when he spoke to the wife of such a domineering master, but it was a chance he was willing to take. Playwright Neil Simon said, "If no one ever took risks, Michelangelo would have painted the Sistine floor." [3] This servant risked speaking to his mistress Abigail as he implored her to do something about the dangerous situation.

Abigail quickly had some of the food gathered that was already prepared for the feast and had it loaded on donkeys; then she headed out to intercept David. When she came upon David and his men, she honored him by kneeling in front of him gently pleading with him to think about what he was about to do. Abigail was able to influence David and prevent the slaughter of her household.

What Lessons Do We Learn From the Young Shepherd?

1. The young shepherd had the courage to speak up for what was right.

Abigail's quick actions prevented David from using his power to destroy her family. However, before she could do that, the servant had to act. You can't fix something if you don't know it's broken. Abigail would not have had the opportunity to intervene if the servant had lacked the courage to tell her what was happening. We should give credit to this young man along with Abigail for stopping David.

When Paul first began his ministry, the Christians had trouble accepting him as a brother; after all, he had been persecuting Christians not so long ago. He had been chasing them down and going from house to house arresting them. Why should they have anything to do with him now? It took someone with the courage of Barnabas to convince the Christians of Paul's sincerity (Acts 9:26-27). Did that take courage for Barnabas to speak up on Paul's behalf? Of course it did. But he knew it was the right thing to do. Do you remember the encouragement the Lord gave to Paul years later when he was on trial in Jerusalem and the Jews were trying to kill him? In Acts 23:11, the Lord said, "Be of good cheer, Paul; for as you have testified for Me in Jerusalem, so you must also bear witness at Rome." Paul was going to need courage to speak up when faced with persecution.

We desperately need that same courage today. Because our world is full of evil, it is critical for Christians to stand up for what is right.

Be of good courage, and He shall strengthen your heart, all you who hope in the LORD. (Psalm 31:24)

We need courage to stand up for what is right, courage to speak out against evil and courage to speak up for Jesus.

2. The young shepherd gave wise advice.

He showed wisdom in his action and in his words when he advised Abigail to think about the situation and do what she thought was right. God's Word is overflowing with references to the blessing of wisdom.

*The mouth of the righteous speaks wisdom,
and his tongue talks of justice. (Psalm 37:30)*

*So that you incline your ear to wisdom, and apply your
heart to understanding. (Proverbs 2:2)*

*Happy is the man who finds wisdom, and the man who gains
understanding; for her proceeds are better than the profits of
silver, and her gain than fine gold. (Proverbs 3:13-14)*

*For wisdom is better than rubies, and all the things one may
desire cannot be compared with her. (Proverbs 8:11)*

*A word fitly spoken is like apples of gold in settings of silver.
Like an earring of gold and an ornament of fine gold is a wise
rebuker to an obedient ear. (Proverbs 25:11-12)*

With the news of an approaching enemy determined to seek retribution still ringing in his ears, this young man seized the opportunity to speak words of wisdom to the listening ear of Abigail. As Christians, we need to be prepared to offer words of wisdom in keeping with God's Word when called upon.

3. The young shepherd was a faithful servant.

He evidently took good care of the sheep, as was his duty, but when his master's family was in danger, he took what steps he could to protect them just as he had protected the sheep. This young man set an example for us that is consistent with God's Word. The word "servant" is used 885 times in the King James Version and 731 times in the New International Version.[4] Abraham, Moses, Samuel, Hannah and David are just a few who are often referred to as servants.

Jesus admonishes us to be faithful servants as well (Mark 10:42-45; John 12:26). Paul specifies how the Lord's servant should act in 2 Timothy 2:22-25. The Easy-to-Read Version reads as follows:

Stay away from the evil things a young person like you typically wants to do. Do your best to live right and to have faith, love, and peace, together with others who trust in the Lord with pure hearts. Stay away from foolish and stupid arguments. You know that these arguments grow into bigger arguments. As a servant of the Lord, you must not argue. You must be kind to everyone. You must be a good teacher, and you must be patient. You must gently teach those who don't agree with you. Maybe God will let them change their hearts so that they can accept the truth.

We don't know much about the young shepherd; we don't even know his name. God's Word does tell us, though, that he had the courage to speak up in a difficult situation; he spoke words of wisdom; and he was a faithful servant – all qualities that we should strive for as we live each day trying to please God.

Let's Think About This

1. Why did the young man go to Abigail instead of Nabal?

2. What do you think this young man's motive was in speaking up? What did he expect to happen?

3. What keeps us from speaking up for Jesus?

4. Do you have a negative or positive impression when you think of the word "servant"? What characteristics should a faithful servant display? Where is it more difficult to have a servant attitude – in your home life, in your job, or in the church?

450 PROPHETS OF BAAL:
Wild and Crazy Guys

1 Kings 16:31-33; 17:1; 18:17-40

One of my favorite TV programs is *Food Network Star*. On the show 12 chefs compete to see which one will win a chance to have his or her own program on the Food Network. The chefs have a limited amount of time to cook amazing dishes using ingredients that I have never even heard of like cuttlefish, durian and salsify. Then they have to face a panel of judges who critique their unique food creations. Each week one contestant is eliminated from the show while another contestant is named that week's winner and is given an advantage over the other competitors for the next challenge. In this lesson we will study not just one man, but 450 men who also were given a huge advantage over their opponent.

In the days of the divided kingdom, Ahab was named king over the 10 tribes of Israel. He was a very sinful king, doing evil in the sight of the Lord, even going so far as to worship the false god Baal. Elijah, the prophet, brought a frightening message for King Ahab from the Lord, telling him that there would be neither dew nor rain until Elijah himself said so. Rain was at that time, and remains today, a very precious commodity in that part of the world, for crops were dependent on the early rains of October and November and the spring rains of March and April.[1] As the prophecy was fulfilled and the rain refused to fall, all the crops dried up, providing no harvest of food for the people and resulting in a severe famine.

Unsung Heroes (and a Few Villains)

In the third year without rain, God told Elijah to deliver a message to King Ahab once again. This time, the message was different; God was going to send rain to end the drought. When Ahab and Elijah met, it was not like two friends greeting one another over a cup of coffee. The tension between them was obvious when Ahab called Elijah "troubler of Israel" (1 Kings 18:17-19). Elijah did not back down from the king's name-calling but accused him of forsaking God in favor of the false gods. Elijah then demanded a gathering of the Israelites with a special invitation for the prophets of Baal and Asherah. Surprisingly, King Ahab agreed to do as Elijah asked.

The word went out and many of the Israelites made their way to Mount Carmel, a mountain range located near the border of Israel and Phoenicia, likely serving as a boundary between the two nations.[2] The mountain had plenty of trees to provide abundant wood for what Elijah had in mind; it was also near the Mediterranean Sea so there would be an ample supply of water. The mountain had rocks and ridges that could be visible from long distances so as to create a "stage" for the Israelites to observe this confrontation.

The Israelites showed up, as did the prophets of Baal. We wonder where the prophets of Asherah were, the idol that represented Baal's wife. No other mention of them appears in Scripture during this event. It is probable that they failed to make an appearance. It turns out that was pretty smart.

Confronting the Israelites regarding their split allegiance to God and Baal, Elijah asked, "Why don't you make up your mind? Who are you going to follow?" They had no answer. How could they? The people were trying to follow Baal to please the king as well as making a half-hearted effort to follow God as their ancestors had. They were probably trying to unite both religions, still worshiping God but also participating in some of the sensuous and impure rites of worship to Baal.[3] We are reminded of the early Christians who tried to combine elements of Judaism with Christianity. Elijah accused the Israelites of "fence-sitting." Because they could not seem to make up their mind regarding who was really God, Elijah suggested a contest to help them decide. This would be no ordinary match-up between Ahab and Elijah; it would be a challenge between God and Baal.[4]

Elijah was not the only prophet of God still alive at this time, much to Queen Jezebel's chagrin; however, he was the only one present on this occasion because the others were hiding in dens and caves to stay out of Jezebel's reach. Here was Elijah, one man representing God, versus 450 prophets showing up on behalf of Baal.

The proposal Elijah made was simple. The prophets of Baal should take a bull, cut it up and place it on an altar with no fire under it, and Elijah would do the same. The Baal prophets would call to their god, and Elijah would call on the name of the Lord, and they would see which one answered by providing fire for the sacrifice. Whichever one could send fire to consume the sacrifice would be the stronger god, the one who could also send the rain and deserved their worship. It sounded like a good plan, and everyone agreed to it.

Although many nations had a local version of a Baal-god, Baal was the principal male god of the Phoenicians and Canaanites. He was considered a sun-god who gave light and warmth to his worshippers, as well as destruction, by the fierce heat of the sun. Archeologists have uncovered rock carvings showing Baal holding a club in his right hand and a lightning flash in his left hand.[5] Because the Canaanites believed that Baal could shoot down lightning flashes from the sky, Elijah's plan gave the followers of Baal an opportunity to show what he could really do. It should have been easy for a sun-god to rain fire.

Elijah generously gave the advantage to the prophets of Baal. They got to go first. They could spend as long as they wanted calling to their god to convince him to send fire on their altar. In 1 Kings 18:26, the New King James Version and New American Standard Bible say they "leaped about the altar," while other versions say they "danced" (NIV), "jumped around" (ERV) or "limped" (ESV). However they did it, the Baal prophets were trying to get the attention of their god. They cried out, "O Baal, hear us!" Imagine the noise as 450 men were all cavorting and shouting. All they got in return, though, was silence. No voice, no fire, no lightning. Nothing. Just stillness. Of course, we know Baal could not answer them because he did not exist. This went on for several hours until about noon when Elijah got tired of just watching and waiting with nothing happening and he decided he would "encourage" them.

Elijah egged them on by saying that possibly they needed to be louder.

Elijah named four reasons their god might not answer them: maybe he was meditating, or busy, or on a journey – or perhaps he was snoozing and they should call louder to wake him up. The *Bible Background Commentary* tells us that the people thought their gods participated in the same activities as humans; thus the prophets of Baal would not have viewed his suggestions as ridiculous or unworthy of deity.[6]

The prophets of Baal were roused to an even greater frenzy by Elijah's words. They even cut themselves, thinking that if the blood of a bull would not move Baal to answer, perhaps their blood might do the trick. Inflicting gashes on themselves was common to many nationalities in that area as a way to please their gods.[7] Even with all this commotion and self-mutilation, Baal did not make an appearance.

Finally Elijah had enough; it was his turn now. First, he repaired the altar of the Lord. Whoever built the original altar in this place is unknown, but it is possible that it was built by people of the northern 10 tribes after the kingdom was divided. Jezebel could have had the altar torn down to promote worship of Baal, for the destruction of competing high places or altars was common during times of religious reformation. Twelve stones were used in rebuilding the altar to remind all the Israelites present that all the tribes should be united in the worship of God.

Elijah erected the altar and then had a trench made around the altar, large enough to hold two measures of seed. Various references deem this amount to be equal to 13 quarts of seed, half a bushel, or 3 gallons. Once the trench was dug, Elijah positioned the wood, cut the bull in pieces, and laid the bull on the wood. Next he had water poured onto the offering. Wow, did he have water poured on it. Four waterpots-full – once, twice, three times! There was so much water that it flowed down and filled the ditch. All this water prevented any suspicion that Elijah might be trying to pull a fast one. No way fire could be concealed under the altar with that much water poured on it. Wait a minute, wasn't there a drought? Where did the water come from? Remember they were near the Mediterranean Sea, which had plenty of water, but it was salt water – not helpful during a drought, but effective for Elijah's purposes.[8] Just imagine what all the people were thinking as they watched this strange display.

The time of the evening sacrifice was probably about 3 o'clock in the afternoon, thus leaving a few hours of daylight for the rest of the day's activities to take place. Elijah lifted his voice to God.

And it came to pass, at the time of the offering of the evening sacrifice, that Elijah the prophet came near and said, "LORD God of Abraham, Isaac, and Israel, let it be known this day that You are God in Israel and I am Your servant, and that I have done all these things at Your word. Hear me, O LORD, hear me, that this people may know that You are the LORD God, and that You have turned their hearts back to You again."
(1 Kings 18:36-37)

What a contrast between the simple prayer of Elijah and the loud pleading of the Baal prophets. We are reminded of Jesus' prayer at the tomb of Lazarus in John 11:41-42 when Jesus prayed aloud so that the people would know the power of God. Elijah wanted the Israelites to remember who was really the One God. The scene was set; it was time to see who was truly worthy of their worship and obedience.

"Then the fire of the LORD fell" (1 Kings 18:38). Throughout Scripture, fire is an indication of the presence of God. We think of the burning bush seen by Moses and the pillar of fire that led the Israelites in the wilderness. Fire also represents acceptance of man's sacrifice. In this case, fire came down, not up, as would usually be the case in a man-made fire. The meat of the bull was first consumed; then the wood was next. The 12 stones and the dust of the altar were even burned up. Nothing could escape the fire from the Lord. The fire even "licked up the water that was in the trench" (v. 38). What a sight to witness! Nobody could deny the power of God after seeing this miraculous event. The Scriptures give us other instances of fire from the Lord in this manner.

> And Moses and Aaron went into the tabernacle of meeting, and came out and blessed the people. Then the glory of the LORD appeared to all the people, and fire came out from before the LORD and consumed the burnt offering and the fat on the altar. When all the people saw it, they shouted and fell on their faces. (Leviticus 9:23-24)

> And David built there an altar to the LORD, and offered
> burnt offerings and peace offerings, and called on the LORD;
> and He answered him from heaven by fire on the altar
> of burnt offering. (1 Chronicles 21:26)

Actually seeing the power of God in such a way brought the people to their knees. Just as Thomas acknowledged Jesus as Lord (John 20:28), the Israelites responded in faith crying out, "The Lord, He is God!" (1 Kings 18:39). The people had finally made their choice; it was God, not Baal, who deserved their allegiance.

Elijah sentenced the prophets of Baal to death, according to God's earlier command in Deuteronomy 18:20 to put to death those people who would have the Israelites follow after other gods. The people were ordered to seize them, and they were executed at the Brook Kishon.

What Lessons Do We Learn From the 450 Prophets of Baal?

1. We must not follow the wrong leader.

It is possible that many, if not most, of the prophets of Baal were Israelites who were familiar with God but chose to follow Baal instead. Perhaps they truly believed in Baal as a god; perhaps they were just trying to please King Ahab and Queen Jezebel. For whatever reason, they opted to be servants of a false god. We must be careful that we don't let any reason cause us to stray from God, not public opinion, nor friends, nor ambition, nor lack of knowledge.

2. We cannot serve two masters.

The Israelites wavered between following God and following the false god Baal. God is not pleased when we are not fully devoted to Him. We cannot serve God and wealth; our loyalties must not be divided. "No one can serve two masters; for either he will hate the one and love the other, or else he will be loyal to the one and despise the other. You cannot serve God and mammon" (Matthew 6:24). God expects our complete allegiance. We cannot serve Him and at the same time try to serve another master. It is our duty to serve only the true God.

3. When presented with the truth, sinners must repent.

Thankfully, the people who had gathered for this contest saw the truth and turned from the worship of Baal, immediately recognizing God as Lord and falling on their faces in worship to Him. When we are faced with our own guilt and sinfulness, our only recourse should be repentance before the One who offers forgiveness, as Peter instructed Simon in Acts 8:22, "Repent therefore of this your wickedness, and pray God if perhaps the thought of your heart may be forgiven you."

4. Worshipers of false gods will be punished.

Death came to these men who worshiped Baal just as it had in the time of Moses when the people worshiped the gold calf (Exodus 32:27-28). The Scriptures warn us of the spiritual death that awaits us if we worship the false gods of this world instead of the one true God.

For the wages of sin is death, but the gift of God is eternal life in Christ Jesus our Lord. (Romans 6:23)

The prophets of Baal failed to recognize God as their Master and Lord. They followed the wrong leader, and it cost them their lives. As Christians, we have only one leader and He is the Lord Jesus Christ; we need to be sure that our allegiance is only to Him.

Let's Think About This

1. What "false gods" can pull us away from God today?

2. How do people try to serve both God and the world?

3. Did the prophets of Baal have the opportunity to turn away from worshiping Baal?

4. What can keep people from coming to God in obedience when they are presented with the truth of His Word?

GEHAZI:
A Servant Who Desired Riches

2 Kings 4:1-37; 5:1-27; 8:4-5

I n his book *Living Above the Level of Mediocrity*, Charles Swindoll describes how the men of the Zulu tribe in Africa catch the ringtailed monkey, a lively little animal that is one of the very hardest animals to trap. The method the Zulus use is based on their knowledge of the animal. Their preferred trap is nothing more than a melon, the seeds of which are a favorite of the ringtailed monkey, growing on a vine. Knowing this, the Zulus simply cut a hole in the melon just large enough for the monkey to insert his hand to reach the seeds inside. The monkey will stick his hand in, grab as many seeds as he can, then start to withdraw it, but he soon finds he cannot take his hand out because his full fist is larger than the hole. The monkey will pull and tug, screech and fight the melon for hours, but he can't get free of the trap unless he gives up the seeds, which he refuses to do. Meanwhile, the Zulus sneak up and nab him; the monkey's greed has cost him his freedom.[1]

During the time of the kings of Israel, the prophet Elisha was much like an old-time traveling preacher, going from one place to another proclaiming God's word. A faithful woman in the town of Shunem often offered this preacher a good home-cooked meal when he passed through the area. One day, she came up with an even better idea. She convinced her husband that they should add a small room to their home and furnish it so that Elisha would be comfortable when he came to town. How generous on their part. How much he must have appreciated having somewhere to lie down and rest. In response to her kindness, Elisha wanted to show this woman his gratitude.

Like many men, Elisha was not sure what he could do for this woman as a gesture of his appreciation. Gehazi was Elisha's trusted servant who accompanied him on his journeys. Elisha had Gehazi speak to the woman, asking what they could do for her in return for her generosity. She humbly did not ask for anything, but a light bulb went off over Gehazi's head, and he had a wonderful idea. Gehazi noted that this couple had no children and thought a child might fulfill the woman's heart's desire. He shared his thoughts with his master. The Shunammite woman was thrilled when Elisha gave her the good news that she would bear a son the next year. It happened just as he said.

Some time later, though, the news was not so joyous when her beloved son became sick and died. After lovingly placing her dead child on the bed of the prophet, she immediately left in search of Elisha. When Elisha sent Gehazi to meet her, she refused to disclose what was wrong; she would trust only Elisha with information this important.

As she neared the man of God, she threw herself at his feet. Gehazi tried to protect his master and push the woman away, but Elisha was willing to listen to her, knowing that her soul was troubled. Elisha realized that her son needed him.

Gehazi was sent on ahead by his master and told to get there fast, not even stopping to greet people along the way. When he arrived, he was to lay the staff of Elisha on the child's face, and Elisha would follow. Gehazi did exactly as he was told, but when he laid the staff on the child's face, there was no response. Nothing happened. Perhaps he was too late. Gehazi left to tell his master that his actions had produced no awakening of the child. Elisha arrived and found the child, lying dead on his bed. After praying to the Lord, Elisha stretched himself out on the boy until life returned and the child opened his eyes. Gehazi was told to summon the child's mother for the happy reunion.

The next time we see Gehazi the story does not have the same happy ending. Israel has an uneasy peace with the country of Syria lying to the north. During one conflict, the Syrians had taken captives, including a young girl from Israel whose name we are never told. She wound up as a servant girl attending to the wife of Naaman, a captain in the Syrian army. Naaman had a serious medical problem; he was a leper.

The word "leprosy" in the Scriptures can be used for various diseases affecting the skin. Evidently Naaman's particular disease was not considered to be contagious because he was not separated from the general population. Possibly he had some other form of skin problem rather than what we think of as full-blown leprosy; modern diagnoses might include psoriasis, eczema, seborrheic dermatitis or fungal-type infections.[2] Still, none of these diseases are pleasant, and the skin lesions may appear in such a way as to repulse others.

No background information is given to us regarding the young servant girl. We don't know exactly where she was from nor do we know her age; we also don't know how long she lived with Naaman and his wife. We know only that she was young; she was from Israel; and she was very brave. This young girl, even though in a servant position, was not afraid to speak to her master's wife. She had enough knowledge to know that the prophet in Samaria could cure Naaman, and she shared that information with his wife. Naaman's wife evidently told her husband what the young girl said.

Naaman passed on this information to the king of Syria. The king sent Naaman to Israel along with gifts and a letter to the king of Israel. The gifts Naaman carried were extremely valuable. Ten talents of silver equaled about 750 pounds and the 6,000 shekels of gold amounted to about 150 pounds. It has been estimated that in today's world, it would be valued at approximately three-quarters of a billion dollars.[3] They also threw in 10 changes of clothing. What does this tell us about Naaman? He must have been considered very important in Syria to warrant this much payment for a cure for his illness. This also tells us that the king of Syria thought he could buy a miracle cure with enough money.

Of course, the king of Israel could not do anything about Naaman's leprosy and was not at all happy about being asked, even tearing his clothes as evidence of his displeasure. Elisha, the prophet, heard about what was happening and sent word that Naaman should be sent to him.

Elisha told Naaman through a servant to wash in the Jordan River seven times and his flesh would be restored to him. But Naaman did not like this order, especially delivered by a mere servant. He wondered why he should do something that seemed so foolish since surely there were better waters in other places where he could wash. He just would not do it. Thankfully Naaman's servants convinced him to give it a try, saying in 2 Kings 5:13, "My father, if the prophet had told you to do something great, would you not have done it? How much more then, when he says to you, 'Wash, and be clean'?" Naaman finally did as Elisha instructed and was rewarded with skin that was free of leprosy. However, this is not the end of the story. Naaman returned and wanted to give a present to Elisha in appreciation for his healing.

God's prophet refused the gift; he desired no monetary payment, realizing that the healing was given by God. Naaman then asked for some soil to take home with him, suggesting that he intended to offer sacrifices to God on an altar built from the dirt from Israel. Elisha sent Naaman away in peace, and this miraculously cleansed army captain and his escorts began their journey back home. Gehazi, Elisha's trusted servant, however, had other ideas. He thought about how Elisha didn't take any gifts from Naaman after healing him. After all, wasn't getting his health back worth something? Gehazi thought that perhaps Naaman would offer him some of the payment he had brought with him that Elisha had refused.

Naaman saw Gehazi running after them and thought something must be wrong. Gehazi told a lie, saying Elisha has sent him to ask for silver and clothes for two young prophets who had just arrived. Compared to what Naaman offered Elisha, this was not a large amount to ask for, but it was still a considerable sum. The silver alone would have amounted to the equivalent of 10 million dollars.[4] Gehazi would have been sitting pretty with that much silver.

Not only did Naaman gladly give what was asked of him, but he also doubled the amount of silver. How little money means when compared to good health. Servants of Naaman even helped Gehazi carry all the loot back. Gehazi secreted the bounty away before going to see Elisha.

> Now he went in and stood before his master. Elisha said to him, "Where did you go, Gehazi?" And he said, "Your servant did not go anywhere." Then he said to him, "Did not my heart go with you when the man turned back from his chariot to

meet you? Is it time to receive money and to receive clothing, olive groves and vineyards, sheep and oxen, male and female servants? Therefore the leprosy of Naaman shall cling to you and your descendants forever." And he went out from his presence leprous, as white as snow. (2 Kings 5:25-27)

Oh, Gehazi! Do you not know better than to lie to a prophet of God? He might have gotten away with lying to Naaman but not to Elisha. He sounded like a child whining, "I didn't do anything." Elisha knew the truth. As punishment, the leprosy of Naaman would cling to Gehazi and his descendants forever.

Surprisingly, we see Gehazi one more time in Scripture when he is standing before the king faithfully recounting stories of the ministry of Elisha. He is still called "the servant of the man of God." Perhaps he repented of his sins in the Naaman affair and continued as Elisha's servant; we are not told if he still had the leprosy at this point. While he was in the middle of telling the king about the restoration of life to the Shunammite woman's son, she suddenly showed up. She had been away a few years and now she wanted her land back. Fortunately for her, Gehazi was able to confirm her identity and the king allowed her to reclaim her property.

What Lessons Do We Learn From Gehazi?
1. The sin of greed can pull a good man down.

First Timothy 6:10 warns that the love of money is the root of all kinds of evil. Money in itself is not evil, but desiring riches above all else can make us lose sight of what is truly important.

For what will it profit a man if he gains the whole world, and loses his own soul? (Mark 8:36-37)

I knew a fine Christian man many years ago who had a good job. Unfortunately, because he wanted what he thought was more out of life, he began drinking with his boss to get on his "good side." He often went out of town because of his job, and he neglected the worship of God. As he progressed up the corporate ladder, his faith meant less and less to him until he finally left God completely. Greed is an ugly monster; it pushes its way into our thoughts and leads us away from God.

2. One sin leads to another.

Gehazi's sin started out with greed when he left his master and ran after Naaman to see what riches he could get for himself. Then he told a lie, even referring to the prophets of God in his dishonest attempt to obtain valuables from Naaman. He cheated Naaman, who trusted him, by accepting silver and garments under false pretenses, and his sin continued to escalate when he told his master Elisha yet another lie. How many of us do something wrong and then try to cover it up with sin upon sin.

King David provides another example of sin spiraling out of control. After David lusted for the beautiful Bathsheba, he committed adultery with her which led him to devise a plan to cover up his sin, resulting in the death of Bathsheba's husband Uriah (2 Samuel 11). Only after the prophet Nathan related to David the story of the neighbor's lamb did David recognize the magnitude of his own sin as he confessed, "I have sinned against the LORD" (2 Samuel 12:13). We must not allow sin to drive us to even greater depths in our lives.

3. We are responsible for our actions even if those around us are righteous.

Gehazi had the privilege of spending time with the faithful prophet Elisha, but the righteousness of others will not save us. Each of us is accountable for our individual behavior. Matthew 16:27 says "For the Son of Man will come in the glory of His Father with His angels, and then He will reward each according to his works." And Romans reminds us "So then each of us shall give account of himself to God" (14:12).

Have you ever heard a husband say, "My wife is good enough for both of us"? Some people live as though they will inherit heaven on the coattails of someone else, but the Scriptures plainly teach that each person is personally responsible for his or her salvation. We cannot depend on the goodness of someone close to us to "rub off" on us. Our eternal destination will be the outcome of our deeds in this life, not the behavior of others.

When we first see Gehazi, he seems to be a faithful servant; however, when the ugliness of greed sweeps over him, he begins a downward spiral of sin. We need to be aware of the strong pull that sin, especially greed, can have on us so that we can fight the temptation to turn away from our Master.

Let's Think About This

1. What sins did Gehazi commit?

2. What effect did these sins have?

3. Name other examples in Scripture of one sin leading to another. How can we keep sin from escalating in our personal lives?

4. How does our society contribute to the temptation of greed?

5. Think of people you know who live as though they are hoping to please God based on the behavior of others. How can we reach those people with God's message?

THE MAN WHO TOUCHED ELISHA'S BONES:
A Second Chance at Life

2 Kings 13:20-21

Funeral customs from ancient times often sound strange to our ears. About 3,000 years ago in China, the now extinct people of Bo came up with a unique way of interring their dead by perfecting the practice of hanging coffins on the sides of mountains or cliffs. The coffins would be lowered from the top of the cliff by ropes to rest on either rock outcrops or wooden stakes wedged into the rock. Almost 100 coffins can still be seen hanging today. Presumably the people of Bo believed the hanging coffins could prevent bodies from being taken by beasts and could bless the souls of the dead eternally because they would be closer to heaven.[1]

If you didn't want to hang on the side of a cliff, perhaps you would have preferred hanging in a tree. Tree burial involved wrapping the body in a shroud or cloth or a simple wooden box and placing it in the crook of a tree to decompose. This custom was practiced by people in Australia, British Columbia and some native North American tribes.[2]

New options for disposing of our bodies after death are available to us today. If you like the idea of being close to nature, a newer version of a "tree burial" may interest you; an environmentally friendly burial is available in which your body is laid to rest under a newly planted tree to serve as compost. If water is more your thing, you may want to consider becoming part of an Eternal Reef where crushed bones left over from cremations are mixed with concrete to create an artificial reef that is placed in water where reefs need restoration to attract fish.[3]

Does cryonics sound to you like something out of a science fiction film? The people at the Cryonics Institute in Michigan don't think so. Cryonics is the process of freezing a person's body hoping that later advances in medical science will make revival possible. The procedure involves cooling legally-dead people to liquid nitrogen temperature where physical decay essentially stops. As of 2014, 126 people have had their bodies frozen at the Cryonics Institute.[4] Although future life is not guaranteed, the scientists involved believe it is a "real possibility."

The Scriptures tell us of another nontraditional burial. The story of the prophet Elisha, often referred to as "the man of God," begins when he was summoned for his new responsibilities as prophet (1 Kings 19:15-16). The prophet Elijah found Elisha plowing a field. By placing his mantle or cloak around the shoulders of Elisha, Elijah demonstrated the calling of Elisha to be his successor. For the next eight years or so, Elisha served as an apprentice to Elijah, ministering to him much as Joshua did to Moses. When it was almost time for God to take Elijah to heaven by a whirlwind, Elijah asked Elisha what he would like done for him (2 Kings 2:9-13). Elisha humbly asked for a double portion of the spirit of Elijah; he would know his request had been granted if he saw Elijah taken from him. When Elisha saw Elijah taken up by a whirlwind to heaven, Elisha cried out, "My father, my father, the chariot of Israel and its horsemen!" (v. 12). Elijah was a powerful prophet and servant of God. Now Elisha would assume that position.

For the next 50 years, Elisha was faithful to God. We have recorded twice as many of Elisha's miracles as those performed by Elijah. Elisha filled the widow's vessels with oil; he restored the life of the Shunammite woman's son; he calmed the poison in the pot of stew; he healed Naaman of leprosy; he made the iron axe-head float. Elisha was friend to both foreigners and Israelites; he was kind and generous as he faithfully served God.

When Elisha was an old man, he fell ill and knew he would soon die. When Joash the king heard the sad news, he visited Elisha and, weeping, said, "O my father, my father, the chariots of Israel and their horsemen!" (2 Kings 13:14). Do those words of King Joash sound familiar? They are the very same words Elisha used at the death of his mentor Elijah. In the next few verses, Elisha counseled Joash one last time regarding what would take place in Israel's future battles with the army of Syria (vv. 14-19). Elisha divulged to King Joash that he would defeat the army of Syria three times in the future, and then Elisha died.

Let's stop for a minute and consider the burial practices of the Israelites at this time in history. Because the Israelites did not normally embalm their dead and because of the hot climate, burial was ordinarily done within a day of death. Bodies were not typically buried in the ground as we think of burial today but were placed on rock shelves or on the floor in caves or chambers cut into soft rock.[5] One archaeological site southwest of the Old City of Jerusalem is Ketef Hinnom where a series of rock-hewn burial chambers based on natural caverns dating back to 650 B.C. has been located. One of the chambers was capable of holding approximately nine bodies on stone benches. After a time the skeletons could be gathered up and piled to one side of the cave to make room for new burials.[6] Many generations of the same family often used the same tomb. Think of Abraham who bought the cave at Machpelah for his beloved Sarah, but other family members were buried there as well (Genesis 49:29-31). Bodies were washed and wrapped in clean cloths along with spices to be buried, but coffins were not used. The dead were sometimes carried on a simple pallet or bier by family members as mourners followed them to the burial site.

So Elisha died and was buried. We are not told any additional details regarding his burial, but surprisingly, that is not the end of his story. God performed one more miracle surrounding Elisha. *Easton's Bible Dictionary* says that a year passed after Elisha's body was placed in its grave.[7] The spring of year came, the time when the crops began to ripen and enemy armies began to attack. Instead of one large invasion, the Moabites often used this time to make small excursions into Samaria by marauding bands or roaming soldiers invading the land and plundering goods.[8]

One day a man died and was being buried; we would say it was the middle of his funeral. Suddenly the pallbearers looked up and saw one of these groups of enemy soldiers nearby. They did not want to be anywhere in the vicinity where these Moabites might attack them so they "got out of Dodge." They left the area in a hurry, but not before tossing the body they were carrying into the closest grave, which happened to be Elisha's. Then the strangest thing happened. When the dead body touched the bones of Elisha, the man's life was restored, and he stood up. I wonder what he thought when he looked around, realized that he was in a burial cave, and saw his friends running away. Can't you just hear the comments of the burial party as they made a quick getaway? "Hey, look, there's our buddy coming out of the tomb!" Do you suppose the man whose life was revived also ran away to escape the Moabites?

Think for a moment about the effect this miraculous occurrence would have had on the Israelites. Their spiritual leader, Elisha, had died; perhaps they were feeling abandoned and alone. Without Elisha to guide them, they may have been full of doubt and discouragement. Was God still with them? Would God continue to bless them without Elisha's presence? Could they still overcome their enemies? Even King Joash may have wondered if Elisha's as yet unfulfilled prophecies would come to pass. Then God used the bones of Elisha to give a man life. Surely this would be the talk of the town! This miracle would let the king, as well as all the people, know that God was still in control and still powerful and that they could continue to trust God. The final prophecies of Elisha came true during the rule of King Joash, providing more proof of God's constant care.

And Hazael king of Syria oppressed Israel all the days of Jehoahaz. But the LORD was gracious to them, had compassion on them, and regarded them, because of His covenant with Abraham, Isaac, and Jacob, and would not yet destroy them or cast them from His presence. Now Hazael king of Syria died. Then Ben-Hadad his son reigned in his place. And Jehoash the son of Jehoahaz recaptured from the hand of Ben-Hadad, the son of Hazael, the cities which he had taken out of the hand of Jehoahaz his father by war. Three times Joash defeated him and recaptured the cities of Israel. (2 Kings 13:22-25)

What Lessons Do We Learn From the Man Who Touched Elisha's Bones?

1. We must not waste second chances.

Wouldn't we love to know more about the man who was restored to life? What was the first thing he did when he left the tomb? Did he run home to his family? How long did he live before death once again took him? Did he remember what happened after death? The one thing we do know is that he was uniquely given a second chance at life. We may daydream about what we would do if we could start life all over again. I once talked with a woman whose daughters were born 20 years apart. She told me that she thought she would do better the second time around, but everything was pretty much the same. If we are fortunate enough to be given a second chance in a friendship, in a family matter, or, more importantly, in our relationship with God, we must not waste that opportunity, for true second chances are rare. We may need to correct previous mistakes; we may need to adjust our attitudes; we may need to change our behavior. What we must not do, though, is squander the opportunity if we are blessed with a second chance.

The story of Jonah is a very familiar one. God instructed Jonah to go to Nineveh to preach, but Jonah wasn't too keen on the idea and hightailed it the other direction. After getting a lesson in obedience from a rather large "teacher" in the sea, Jonah was blessed to receive a second chance (Jonah 3:1-3). Jonah used this second opportunity to preach repentance to the Ninevites.

The Lord is not slack concerning His promise, as some count slackness, but is longsuffering toward us, not willing that any should perish but that all should come to repentance. (2 Peter 3:9)

God gives us second chances, third chances – and even more. We must be careful not to waste these golden opportunities.

2. A blessing sometimes comes when all hope is gone.

The friends of this dead man were expecting to bury him; his family was ready to say their final goodbyes. They had no hope of seeing him alive again, of ever being able to talk to him or walk by his side once more. We cannot expect God to bring our loved ones back to life as He did on this occasion, but we do sometimes receive blessings when we think all hope is gone. Have you ever given up on a rebellious teenager only to have her turn her life back to God? Perhaps you thought your marriage was nearing the end when your husband finally agreed to counseling and you were able to re-establish your marriage; maybe you were lonely and a friend called and brightened your day. In Philippians, we read of Paul in prison in Rome, awaiting trial and possible execution. He continued to trust God and be joyful even though the situation looked bleak, and then Epaphroditus arrived from Philippi with support from his Philippian brethren (Philippians 4:18). What a blessing! What a lift to his spirits! God is gracious and sends us blessings when we need them most.

3. A righteous life can affect someone "dead" in sin.

Do you think the man would have been restored to life if his body had touched someone else's bones? His life was revived by coming in contact with the bones of this man of God. When people today are dead in sin, they can find new life by coming in contact with faithful Christians. Our impact on sinners must never be underestimated because the influence of our lives can have eternal significance. The people we see everyday can be touched by how we treat them. When the woman with the flow of blood touched the garment of Jesus in Matthew 9, she was healed and her life was never the same. In much the same way, we can affect those who come in contact with us each day. As we teach them about Christ, we can help them learn how to be cleansed from their sins so that their lives will be different.

The Television Academy Hall of Fame once honored Fred Rogers of *Mister Rogers' Neighborhood*. Rogers made an inspiring speech telling the people working in the TV industry that they had the opportunity to encourage people either to demean life or cherish it.[9] Our opportunity as Christians is even greater, for we can encourage people to know Christ.

4. The dead man was given new life by our Almighty God.

For the living know that they will die; but the dead know nothing, and they have no more reward, for the memory of them is forgotten. Also their love, their hatred, and their envy have

*now perished; nevermore will they have a share in anything
done under the sun. (Ecclesiastes 9:5-6)*

The dead are just that – dead. Even though Elisha had performed
miracles during his lifetime, that power died with him. Elisha could not
possibly have done this on his own. The man's life was restored, not
by Elisha or even his bones, but by the loving hand of God. Aren't we
thankful that God will also give us new life? First John 5:11 reminds
us: "And this is the testimony: that God has given us eternal life, and
this life is in His Son." We have a new life waiting for us through the
grace of God; the life-giving power of God is there for each of us if we
will lay our lives at His feet.

We don't know much about this man who was restored to life. We
don't know his family or his hometown or anything about his life;
however, from his story we can be reminded that our God is a God of
second chances, that He is willing to bless us even in our darkest hours,
that we can touch the lives of those dead in sin, and that our God is
mighty and willing to give us new life as well.

Let's Think About This

1. What second chances has God given you in life?

2. How do you think the dead man's family might have reacted upon
   seeing him alive again?

3. What should our attitude be toward people who need to be given
   another chance in this life?

4. Name other men and women in the Bible who were given a second
   chance.

KING MANASSEH:
The Boy Who Wore a Crown
2 Kings 21:1-8; 2 Chronicles 33:1-20

The whole world held its breath, knowing this would be a historic day. The press had been staked out around the clock for over a week waiting for this moment. Photographers stood on stepladders with camera equipment perched and focused so as not to miss a single shot. The time finally arrived and the announcement immediately went out around the world that a new royal baby had been born in London. On July 22, 2013, Prince William and Catherine, the Duke and Duchess of Cambridge, became the proud parents of a future king whom they named George Alexander Louis. Third in line to the throne after his grandfather and father, this baby boy will grow up knowing that he will someday become king of Great Britain.

In much the same way, sons have had kingdoms handed down from their fathers since Bible times. Sometimes the heirs had the qualities and characteristics to be good rulers, but often a son deviated from the path his father had walked.

The Israelites, God's people, could not get along and finally split into two kingdoms. Ten of the tribes became the kingdom of Israel; the other two tribes formed the kingdom of Judah. Each kingdom had its own king and its own territory. One of the kings was Manasseh, the 14th king of Judah, who took over the throne at the tender age of 12. Manasseh was the only son of Hezekiah, one of the so-called "good" kings of Judah and grandson of Ahaz, one of Judah's most wicked kings. Manasseh was born about three years after Hezekiah had been miraculously healed by God and given an additional 15 years to live.[1] Although we are not privy to much information about King Manasseh's time in power, he reigned for 55 years, longer than any other king in Israel or Judah. Unfortunately, King Manasseh failed to follow in his father's footsteps but instead reverted to the ways of his evil grandfather.

God had forced out the peoples in the land of Canaan because they did not honor Him as Lord, and now Manasseh was leading God's people down that very same path. Manasseh practiced many of the same evils as the nations that God had cast out.

Manasseh re-established the high places that his father had destroyed, places for worship that were often on hills and mountains and frequently used to worship false gods. King Manasseh went so far as to build altars for the false gods of the Canaanite people such as Baal and Asherah. He erected altars on which they could burn incense to worship the stars in the heavens, even placing such altars in the courtyards of the Lord's temple. Second Kings 21:6 gives us the horrifying fact that he sacrificed his son by burning him on an altar. Manasseh also tried to know the future by contacting mediums and wizards. All of this was in direct opposition to the commands of the Lord.

> When you come into the land which the LORD your God is giving you, you shall not learn to follow the abominations of those nations. There shall not be found among you anyone who makes his son or his daughter pass through the fire, or one who practices witchcraft, or a soothsayer, or one who interprets omens, or a sorcerer, or one who conjures spells, or a medium, or a spiritist, or one who calls up the dead. For all who do these things are an abomination to the LORD, and because of these abominations the LORD your God drives them out from before you. (Deuteronomy 18:9-12)

Manasseh brought wickedness to a whole new level among the Israelites, making the Lord very angry.

God had earlier chosen Jerusalem to be His special city with His temple and abiding place located there. God instructed that as long as

His people continued to obey Him, He would bless them, but Manasseh persisted in leading them away from God. Manasseh even placed a statue of Asherah, a Canaanite goddess, in God's holy temple, thus desecrating the temple. It seems that every religion was tolerated except the worship of God. Instead of being revolted by the lifestyle of the Canaanites, the king lived in the same sinful manner as the Canaanite people whom God had earlier destroyed.

Our loving God did not forsake His people but sent prophets to turn them back to Him. We are not told the names of these particular prophets, but because this was during the time that Hosea, Joel, Nahum, Habakkuk and Isaiah were prophesying, God certainly could have used these men.[2] Through the prophets, God admonished His people that misfortune was on the way, using figurative language to warn that God would bring calamity so terrible that whoever heard of it, "both his ears will tingle" (2 Kings 21:12). According to the *Bible Exposition Commentary*, the Hebrew word meaning "to tingle" is related to the word for cymbals and bells.[3] When they heard the disaster was coming, it would be like hearing a sudden clash of cymbals. But it would be too late.

Other startling images were used to try to make them understand the significance of the trouble that was coming. The "measuring line of Samaria" (2 Kings 21:13) would be stretched over Jerusalem. Workers would use a string with a rock or weight on it to mark a straight line at the end of a stone wall, and any stones outside the line were chipped off and thrown away. This vivid word picture showed how God would "throw away" the kingdom of Judah precisely as He had Samaria and Ahab's family of kings. The last illustration comes from the kitchen. Just as we wipe all the water out of a plate after washing it, God would "wipe out" the kingdom of Judah (v. 13). God would abandon them just as they had deserted God. These final tribes would be turned over to their enemies.

Manasseh deserved such severe punishment from God because of all the evil he did in shedding innocent blood. The historian Josephus (Ant.10:3, sec.1) writes that Manasseh slew many righteous men and prophets so that Jerusalem flowed with their blood.[4] Tradition states that Manasseh even had the prophet Isaiah sawn in two with a wooden saw.[5] This king of Judah was certainly a most wicked man.

Unsung Heroes (and a Few Villains)

In 2 Kings 21:17-18, Manasseh's death and burial are given as a simple statement of fact; thus, the writer of 2 Kings relates in a mere 18 verses the history of Manasseh and his 55-year reign. But that is not all the story. To grasp the complete story, we must also read the narrative in 2 Chronicles.

In 2 Chronicles 33:1-9, we are given pretty much the same account we had in 2 Kings relating to King Manasseh; however, beginning in verse 10 we find out more about his time as King of Judah. God spoke to Manasseh and his people, warning them over and over, but they refused to listen, simply ignoring God and doing what they wanted. Now it was time to get Manasseh's attention; it was time for judgment from God. This would have been approximately during the 22nd year of Manasseh's reign.

God often used the armies of other nations to exact punishment on the Israelites. On this particular occasion when the Lord brought the Assyrian army down on them, one of those captured was King Manasseh himself. When kings were made captive, they were usually treated with great cruelty. They "took Manasseh with hooks, bound him with bronze fetters, and carried him off to Babylon" (2 Chronicles 33:11). *Easton's Bible Dictionary* tells us that they were brought before the conqueror with a hook or ring passed through their lips or their jaws that had a cord attached to it; thus they were led around like cattle.[6] Manasseh was kept as a prisoner for an unspecified period of time in Babylon, the seat of the Assyrian government at that time.

What a plummet for this powerful king. He was no longer treated as royalty, a man who enjoyed riches and power, but he was now a prisoner in a foreign land, despised and brutally treated. As horrifying as his incarceration must have been, the ultimate outcome of his suffering was a blessing.

In his captivity, King Manasseh finally turned to God, humbling himself and entreating the Lord. What a joy when suffering brings one to repentance. Paul must have had this in mind when he wrote the letter to the Christians at Corinth.

> Now I rejoice, not that you were made sorry, but that your sorrow led to repentance. For you were made sorry in a godly

manner, that you might suffer loss from us in nothing. For godly sorrow produces repentance leading to salvation, not to be regretted; but the sorrow of the world produces death. (2 Corinthians 7:9-10)

Suffering can bring about godly grief which leads to repentance. Manasseh suffered, and his distress made him realize how much he needed the Lord. Thankfully, Manasseh was not too proud to humble himself before God, praying to Him, not the false idols he had been worshiping, and begging for God's help. Our gracious God was touched by Manasseh's pleading and answered his prayer, bringing him out of captivity although we are not given any details regarding his deliverance. Not only was he a free man again, but he also was restored to his throne in Jerusalem. The Scriptures tell us: "Then Manasseh knew that the LORD was God" (2 Chronicles 33:13). Finally Manasseh recognized God Almighty as his true Master, and like Saul on the road to Damascus, his eyes were opened to the truth. When he acknowledged God, Manasseh set about making things right.

King Manasseh tried to restore the city, rebuilding the outer wall and assigning army officers to the fortified cities. More importantly, he removed the false gods and idols from the temple and destroyed the altars to these strange gods. The king reinstituted worship on the altar of the Lord and began once more offering sacrifices in accordance with the Law of God. Although the reform might not have converted the entire nation, Manasseh at least restored the worship of the true God.

What Lessons Do We Learn From King Manasseh?

1. Sin is wrong even if everyone else is doing it.

Wrong is wrong, even if it is commonly considered acceptable. Exodus 23:2 emphatically states, "You shall not follow a crowd to do evil." That couldn't be any plainer. Just because everyone else is committing a sin doesn't make it right. As mothers say, "Just because everyone else is jumping off a bridge doesn't mean you have to!" King Manasseh saw all the nations around the Israelites worshiping false gods, and instead of standing firm in his support of the one true God, he decided to go along with everyone else.

Unsung Heroes (and a Few Villains)

How hard is it for us to remain faithful to God, to keep from sin, when we are surrounded by sins every day? The fact that multiple people approve of something does not make it right. This is where our influence as Christians is especially important. If we just go along with the crowd, even in wrongdoing, we will never win the world for Christ.

2. Sometimes bad things happen to make us realize our need for God.

When Hannah's desire for a baby had been denied, she went to the house of the Lord and poured out her deepest longings to God, knowing that only God could fulfill her yearning (1 Samuel 1:10). Paul often faced death due to his preaching of the truth; consequently his hardship made him trust in God all the more (2 Corinthians 1:9-10).

When my life is pretty rosy, when everything is rocking right along with no problems, it is easy to become dependent on myself. I might think, "I have everything under control. I am doing pretty well for myself. I don't need any help." Then when trouble comes, I am brought to my knees. I finally grasp my need for God in my life and I turn to Him just as Manasseh did.

3. Change is possible even for the worst of sinners.

We are told repeatedly in Scripture that Manasseh did more evil than the nations God had previously destroyed for their sins. Even though Manasseh knew God, he chose to worship false gods; he set up idols; he even sacrificed the life of one of his sons to a false deity. After all that, he eventually came back to God; he put aside the sin in his life and renewed his faith and allegiance to the true and living God. We are reminded again of Paul who called himself the worst of sinners, yet he was given mercy when he turned to Christ:

> This is a faithful saying and worthy of all acceptance, that Christ Jesus came into the world to save sinners, of whom I am chief. However, for this reason I obtained mercy, that in me first Jesus Christ might show all longsuffering, as a pattern to those who are going to believe on Him for everlasting life. (1 Timothy 1:15-16)

I wonder if we had met Paul or Manasseh, while they were living as sinners, whether we would have tried to teach them how to live as

God commands. Or would we have thought they were too far gone? We must be careful that we do not make judgment calls about which sinners we will try to teach. Only God knows a man's heart. It is not up to us to judge whether a man will receive the truth; our responsibility to teach the gospel.

4. God is always willing to forgive if we will come to Him.

In Him we have redemption through His blood, the forgiveness of sins, according to the riches of His grace. (Ephesians 1:7)

If we confess our sins, He is faithful and just to forgive us our sins and to cleanse us from all unrighteousness. (1 John 1:9)

We are never beyond God's love and mercy. God has promised to forgive us of our sins if we will obey Him, and God keeps His promises faithfully.

5. Even if we repent, we may still suffer consequences for our sins.

We can have the forgiveness of God but still suffer the effects of sin in our lives. King Manasseh had to live the rest of his life knowing he had killed one or more of his children in sacrifice to a false god. How horrible to live with that knowledge. He also had to accept that his evil actions influenced his surviving son, Amon.

> Amon was twenty-two years old when he became king, and he reigned two years in Jerusalem. His mother's name was Meshullemeth the daughter of Haruz of Jotbah. And he did evil in the sight of the LORD, as his father Manasseh had done. So he walked in all the ways that his father had walked; and he served the idols that his father had served, and worshiped them. He forsook the LORD God of his fathers, and did not walk in the way of the LORD. (2 Kings 21:19-22)

Of course, Manasseh's actions also led an untold number of Israelites away from God and resulted in the death of many. Manasseh repented, but the results of his wicked past could not be undone. The same holds true for us today as the consequences of sin may linger in our lives as well.

King Manasseh serves as an example to us of how wickedness can overtake our lives, but we should also learn from his humility as he recognized his failures. Aren't we thankful for a God who is willing to offer us grace and mercy even in our darkest hour?

Let's Think About This

1. How do we react to lifestyles that differ from those that are pleasing to God?

2. What sins are considered acceptable by society today?

3. Share a time when circumstances helped reinforce your need for God.

4. Do we really believe that change is possible for sinners today? How does believing that people can change affect our spiritual lives?

5. As Christians, do we sometimes have a hard time accepting the forgiveness of God? Why?

6. What sins do people commit today that have consequences even after repentance?

7. How do we help people to cope with the consequences of sin and continue to live a faithful life of obedience to God?

Prov 22:6
Manasseh parents → Hezekiah
& Abijah
(daughter of
Zechariah)

EBED-MELECH: ~King's
Beyond the Call of Duty servant
Jeremiah 37; 38:1-13; 39:15-18 → Ethiopian

Luke 17:7-10 → do your duty & don't expect praise for it

It was a cold night in New York City – Nov. 14, 2012. The frigid weather was particularly distressing for a homeless man who had no shoes. NYPD Officer Larry DePrimo happened to come across this man leaning against the wall near the entrance to a shoe store, barefoot. DePrimo did not tell the homeless man to move along or issue him a citation for loitering. Rather, DePrimo entered the shoe store and bought the man a pair of size 12 all-weather boots and thermal socks. When he came out of the store, DePrimo knelt down and helped the cold man put them on. A tourist from out of town captured the episode on her cell phone camera and posted it online for the whole world to see. DePrimo became famous overnight for his compassionate actions that went far beyond the call of duty.[1]

God had a special job for a man named Jeremiah, who, even before his birth, was chosen to be a prophet to warn the nation of Judah about the coming destruction of Jerusalem (Jeremiah 1:5). For 40 years, he spoke only gloom and doom. Needless to say, he was not very popular. Because of his dire predictions, he became known as "the prophet of doom" and "the weeping prophet."[2]

Jeremiah was prophesying during the time that Zedekiah was king of Judah. Although King Zedekiah had been ruling over Judah for eight years, he had been forced to pay tribute to Nebuchadnezzar, the king of Babylon, during this period. Judah had been allowed by Nebuchadnezzar to remain an independent nation but only under Nebuchadnezzar's authority. After eight long years of this, in the ninth year of his reign, Zedekiah rebelled and asked Egypt for help in freeing Judah from Babylon's control. Nebuchadnezzar heard of it and sent an army to attack Judah. Although Jerusalem didn't completely fall, things were not looking good. Jeremiah 37:5 refers to the Chaldeans besieging Jerusalem. It is important to understand that the Chaldeans, from the southern portion of Babylon, represented the prominent population of the area so the term "Chaldeans" became synonymous with "Babylonians."[3]

Surprisingly, because the kingdom of Judah was not very faithful to God at this time, King Zedekiah sent messengers to Jeremiah to have him pray to the Lord regarding the situation. King Zedekiah sounded like he was really on the fence when it came to serving God. He didn't listen to the words of the Lord; he didn't pay any attention to what Jeremiah said, but he still wanted Jeremiah to go to the Lord on Judah's behalf.

Meanwhile, Egypt's army approached to help the Israelites. The Babylonian army broke off from attacking Jerusalem and evidently turned to do battle with the Egyptian soldiers. The word of the Lord came to Jeremiah telling him that this was only a temporary reprieve. In the end, the Chaldeans would destroy Jerusalem.

During a time of relative peace in the land, Jeremiah went to the area of his hometown to see about some property there. This truly was an innocent trip with no political undertones. Unfortunately, a captain of the guard falsely accused him of being a traitor, trying to go over to the side of the enemy, to the Chaldeans. Ignoring Jeremiah's protests, the authorities had Jeremiah arrested, beaten and put into a dungeon where he stayed for many days. *Jer 37:10*

King Zedekiah had a desire to hear from the Lord once again and had Jeremiah taken from the prison and brought to him. Jeremiah reiterated his earlier prophecy: "You shall be delivered into the hand of the king of Babylon!" (Jeremiah 37:17). Jeremiah also begged that he not be returned to the terrible dungeon where he had been imprisoned. In response to his plea, the king ordered that Jeremiah be kept in the courtyard, evidently a less objectionable alternative to the dungeon. The courtyard was apparently in a section of the king's palace which may have been more like house arrest.

Jeremiah was allowed to continue speaking to the Israelites during this imprisonment, but, again, the people didn't like what they heard. When you don't like the message, kill the messenger. The officials listed in Jeremiah 38:1-4 persuaded the king to let them kill Jeremiah. Regrettably, King Zedekiah was too much of a weakling to deny them. He had the authority to stop them, but he just didn't have the nerve. The king gave Jeremiah into their hands to do with him whatever they chose (v. 5).

Jeremiah was taken and thrown into a cistern where they probably expected him to starve to death.[4] In this dry area of the world where water was always scarce, there would have been a large cistern in every house to hold water. This cistern in the king's house now held no water, only mud and gunk. Can you imagine how uncomfortable Jeremiah would have been? The Bible says, "Jeremiah sank in the mire" (Jeremiah 38:6). It would be interesting to know why they let Jeremiah down with ropes instead of just throwing him in. *Jer 38:6—13*

Now we get down to the man in our study, Ebed-Melech. The name "Ebed-Melech" means "the king's servant"[5] so this may have been more a title than a name. Ebed-Melech was an Ethiopian from Africa; thus he was a Gentile eunuch serving in the king's palace. The news grapevine must have been flourishing back then, for he heard that Jeremiah had been placed in the cistern. When he heard the news, Ebed-Melech didn't hesitate but immediately sought out the king. The king was not currently in the palace but was sitting in the Gate of Benjamin, possibly holding court. Ebed-Melech didn't mince words as he accused the men who took Jeremiah of acting wickedly, voicing his concern for the very life of Jeremiah as long as he was in the cistern.

King Zedekiah did an immediate about-face. Have you ever heard one side of an argument and thought, "Yes, that's right," and then heard the other side and agreed with it? It sounds like Zedekiah is agreeing with whomever is the last one to speak with him. The king commanded Ebed-Melech to take 30 men and bring Jeremiah from the cistern. Why did he need 30 men? It certainly would not have taken 30 men to pull one man out of the mud, but a large number of men would have provided protection from Jeremiah's enemies during his rescue.

Ebed-Melech didn't waste any time in carrying out his task, but before he rescued Jeremiah, he first made one stop in a storeroom where he obtained old, worn-out rags. Ebed-Melech carried these rags to the cistern and let them down by ropes to Jeremiah. Why did he not just throw them down for Jeremiah to catch? Perhaps he didn't want them to land in the mud; maybe Jeremiah was too weak at this point to catch them; it may have been too dark for Jeremiah to see them if they were thrown down. Ebed-Melech kindly lowered the rags and instructed Jeremiah to place them under his armpits to prevent rope burns and then to put the ropes in place so he could be pulled up. Jeremiah probably eagerly did as he was told in his joy at being rescued. The men pulled him up and out, and Jeremiah was safe once again, after which he was remanded back to the court of the guardhouse.

We read of Ebed-Melech only one additional time in Scripture. In Jeremiah 39:15-18, we are told of God's response to Ebed-Melech's actions regarding Jeremiah. Jerusalem would be destroyed by the Babylonians as previously prophesied, but God would spare the life of Ebed-Melech because of his trust in God as evidenced by his actions toward Jeremiah.

2 Kings 22:1-2; 2 Chron 34:1-7

What Lessons Do We Learn From Ebed-Melech?

1. Sometimes immediate action is required.

Matthew Henry wrote in his commentary: "No time must be lost when life is in danger ... ."[6] Ebed-Melech didn't hesitate to act, even though he was going against the officials in King Zedekiah's court. Ebed-Melech understood the urgency of the situation because any delay might have meant the death of Jeremiah.

Have you ever been in a situation where immediate action was required? I went to the mailbox one day and noticed my neighbor and her toddler in their yard across the street. The little boy saw me, too, and quickly started running across the road to say hello. His mother was horrified at seeing her child in the street and loudly called his name. In confusion, he stopped right where he was – in the middle of the street – and turned to look at her. Suddenly, we all saw the car coming toward us. His mother hurriedly ran to her son, scooped him up and carried him to safety. Delay could have been disastrous; she needed to act quickly to protect her son.

Immediate action was required instead of hesitation. If we see someone in trouble, physically or spiritually, we need to act.

2. Ebed-Melech helped when no one else would.

Where were the Israelites, Jeremiah's people, when he was facing death in the pit? Would not one of them step up to try to save his life? Ebed-Melech was an Ethiopian, a foreigner, yet he showed more bravery and compassion than any of Jeremiah's countrymen.

Sometimes we are placed in a situation where we are the only ones who will speak up, the only ones who will step forward to try to remedy a wrong. Perhaps God has placed us at a particular place at a particular time to open the door for us to act. Do you remember what Mordecai asked Esther in Esther 4:14? "Yet who knows whether you have come to the kingdom for such a time as this?" We may be given the opportunity to step up and take action. *Gen 50:20*

3. Ebed-Melech spoke boldly to the king.

What courage Ebed-Melech had. He probably was in danger of losing his position for speaking up because the king was the ultimate authority, but Ebed-Melech stood up to the king and pointed out the wrongdoing. *Fausset's Bible Dictionary* calls this Ebed-Melech's "courageous interference."[7] Do we have such courage?

4. Ebed-Melech showed great compassion.

Like the New York City police officer, Ebed-Melech went beyond the call of duty. He not only rescued Jeremiah from the cistern, but he was thoughtful enough to provide rags for his comfort as he was being pulled out. I love when the Scriptures give us these little details. Ebed-Melech was not only brave but also kind in his dealing with Jeremiah.

Of course, we also have the example of Jesus, our compassionate Savior, who showed kindness to the blind, the sick and the hungry (Matthew 14:14; 20:29-34). As Christians we are commanded to be a compassionate people. Colossians 3:12 tells us, "Therefore, as the elect of God, holy and beloved, put on tender mercies, kindness, humility, meekness, longsuffering." Ebed-Melech certainly illustrates these qualities for us.

We have all heard of people doing random acts of kindness for others. Glenna, one of the ladies at our church, wanted to encourage us to be kinder and more compassionate in our dealings with others and to give God the glory for our actions. She printed up cards for us to hand out as we did good deeds for others. The cards read: "You've been rack'ed! Random Acts of Christian Kindness." Faithful Ebed-Melech performed an act of kindness and in so doing left us an example to follow.

5. Ebed-Melech trusted in God and was rewarded for it.

Ebed-Melech evidently knew Jeremiah was a true prophet of God and trusted God to help him save Jeremiah. Perhaps he had learned to trust God from Jeremiah himself (Jeremiah 17:7-8). Because of his actions and faith in God, the life of Ebed-Melech would be spared when Jerusalem was defeated.

Daniel was also in a dangerous situation when he was thrown into a den of hungry lions, and he, too, was spared because of his trust in God (Daniel 6:23). Solomon tells us in Proverbs 3:5: "Trust in the LORD with all your heart, and lean not on your own understanding." Paul wrote to the Corinthians regarding the despair he felt at his sufferings, but also of his trust in God who raises the dead (2 Corinthians 1:8-9). Ebed-Melech trusted God, and we should as well.

The story of Ebed-Melech is one of courage, kindness and faith in God. This foreign servant teaches us to reach out to others in compassion, even in difficult circumstances. God blessed Ebed-Melech for his "courageous interference," and He will surely bless us as well as we boldly serve Him.

Let's Think About This

1. Have you ever hesitated to act in a situation where immediate action was required? What was the outcome?

2. What keeps us from stepping up to help others? Do we sometimes refrain from speaking up because "it's really none of our business" or "someone else will handle it"?

3. Has intervening become more dangerous in our society today? What guidelines should we keep in mind when considering "courageous interference"?

4. Are we a compassionate people? Do people see Christ in our actions? Name specific works where we can show our compassion to the world.

Zedekiah, son of Josiah.

Endnotes

Chapter 1

1 Andrew Robert Fausset, "Ishmael," *Fausset's Bible Dictionary*, PC Study Bible V5, (Biblesoft, Inc., 1988-2013).

2 William Baur, "Ishmael," *International Standard Bible Encyclopedia*, PC Study Bible V5, (Biblesoft, Inc., 1988-2013).

3 Roswell Dwight Hitchcock, "Ishmael," *Hitchcock's Bible Names Dictionary*, PC Study Bible V5, (Biblesoft, Inc., 1988-2013).

4 Matthew George Easton, "Wean," *Easton's Bible Dictionary*, PC Study Bible V5, Biblesoft, Inc. 1988-2013).

5 Unknown author, Motivation Quotes, <http://zaibiquotes4u.blogspot.com/2013/04/MotivationalQuotes_2343.html>. 10 August 2013.

6 Fausset.

7 *Voltaire*, Brainy Quotes, <http://www.brainyquote.com/quotes/quotes/v/voltaire399440.htmlI#IEIMh4SBO5lm28yo.99, 2001-2013>. 10 August 2013.

Chapter 2

1 *Academy Award*, Wikipedia, <http://en.wikipedia.org/wiki/Academy_Award>. 22 Dec 2013.

2 Benjamin Reno Downer, "Hur," *International Standard Bible Encyclopaedia*, PC Study Bible V5, (Biblesoft, Inc., 1988-2013).

3 Thomas Nelson, "Amalekites," *Nelson's Illustrated Bible Dictionary*, PC Study Bible V5, (Biblesoft, Inc., 1988-2013).

4 John H. Walton, Victor H. Matthews, and Mark W. Chavalas, *The IVP Bible Background Commentary: Old Testament*, (Downers Grove, Ill.: InterVarsity Press, 2000) 92.

Chapter 3

1 Jeanne Robertson, "Don't send a man to the grocery store!", JeanneRobertson.com, 7:53, <http://jeannerobertson.com/MeetingPlannerVideo.htm>. 29 Dec. 2013.

2 Roswell Dwight Hitchcock, "Ithamar," *Hitchcock's Bible Names Dictionary*, PC Study Bible V5, (Biblesoft, Inc., 1988-2013).

3 Albert Barnes, "1 Kings 2:27," *Barnes' Notes*, PC Study Bible V5, (Biblesoft, Inc., 1988-2013).

4 Warren W. Wiersbe, "The Gifted People Give Their Service (Exodus 35:30-39:43)," *Wiersbe's Expository Outlines on the Old Testament*, PC Study Bible V5, (Biblesoft, Inc., 1988-2013).

5 Barnes, "1 Corinthians 14:33"

6 "Dear Lord and Father of Mankind," <http://www.cyberhymnal.org/htm/d/e/dearlord.htm>. 30 Nov. 2014..

7 Charles Swindoll, *Come Before Winter*, (Portland, Oregon: Multnomah Press 1985) 24-25.

Chapter 4

1 Ignaz Semmelweis, History Learning Site, <http://historylearningsite.co.uk/ignaz_semmelweis.htm>. 29 Nov. 2014.

2 Joseph Lister, History Learning Site, <http://www.historylearningsite.co.uk/joseph_Lister.htm>. 29 Nov. 2014.

3 Thomas Nelson, "Tribe," *Nelson's Illustrated Bible Dictionary*, PC Study Bible V5, (Biblesoft, Inc., 1988-2013).

4 John H. Walton, Victor H. Matthews, and Mark W. Chavalas, *The IVP Bible Background Commentary: Old Testament*, (Downers Grove, ILL: InterVarsity Press, 2000) 150.

5 Harold L. Willmington, "Caleb," *Willmington's Bible Handbook*, PC Study Bible V5, (Biblesoft, Inc., 1988-2013).

6 CBS News, <http://www.cbsnews.com/news/poll-53-of-americans-support-same-sex-marriage/>. 29 Dec. 2013.

7 *Abortion*, Gallup, <http://www.gallup.com/poll/1576/abortion.aspx>. 29 Dec. 2013.

Chapter 5

1 *The Mutiny on HMS Bounty, National Museum of the Royal Navy (Portsmouth)*, <http://www.royalnavalmuseum.org/info_sheets_bounty.htm>. 29 Nov. 2014.

2 *Primogeniture*, Merriam-Webster.com, <http://www.merriam-webster.com/dictionary/primogeniture>. 11 Nov. 2013.

3 Thomas Lewis, "Censer," *International Standard Bible Encyclopaedia*, PC Study Bible V5, (Biblesoft, Inc., 1988-2013).

4 Matthew George Easton, "Censer," *Easton's Bible Dictionary*, PC Study Bible V5, (Biblesoft, Inc., 1988-2013).

5 Robert Jamieson, A.R. Fausset and David Brown, "Numbers 16:16-18," *Jamieson, Fausset, and Brown Commentary*, PC Study Bible V5, (Biblesoft, Inc., 1988-2013).

6 Albert Barnes, "Numbers 16:11," *Barnes' Notes*, PC Study Bible V5, (Biblesoft, Inc., 1988-2013).

7 Jamieson, Fausset, and Brown, "Numbers 16:12-14."

Chapter 6

1 Roswell Dwight Hitchcock, "Achan," *Hitchcock's Bible Names Dictionary*, PC Study Bible V5, (Biblesoft, Inc., 1988-2013).

2 John H. Walton, Victor H. Matthews, and Mark W. Chavalas, *The IVP Bible Background Commentary: Old Testament*, (Downers Grove, Ill.: InterVarsity Press, 2000) 218.

3 Albert Barnes, "Joshua 7:3," *Barnes' Notes*, PC Study Bible V5, (Biblesoft, Inc., 1988-2013).

4 Warren W. Wiersbe, "A disobedient soldier (Joshua 7:1, 20-21)," *The Bible Exposition Commentary: Old Testament*, PC Study Bible V5, (Biblesoft, Inc., 1988-2013).

5 Walton, Matthews, and Chavalas, 219.

6 Barnes, "Joshua 7:14."

7 Adam Clarke, "Joshua 7:21," *Adam Clarke's Commentary*, PC Study Bible V5, (Biblesoft, Inc., 1988-2013).

8 Walton, Matthews, and Chavalas, 219.

9 Walton, Matthews, and Chavalas, 219.

Chapter 7

1 John H. Walton, Victor H. Matthews, and Mark W. Chavalas, *The IVP Bible Background Commentary: Old Testament*, (Downers Grove, Ill.: InterVarsity Press, 2000) 277.

2 Walton, Matthews, and Chavalas, 277.

3 Walton, Matthews, and Chavalas, 277.

4 Warren W. Wiersbe, "Ruth prepared to meet Boaz. (Ruth 3:1-5)," *The Bible Exposition Commentary: Old Testament*, PC Study Bible V5, (Biblesoft, Inc., 1988-2013).

5 Wiersbe, "Ruth submitted to Boaz. (Ruth 3:6-9)."

6 Robert Jamieson, A.R. Fausset and David Brown, "Ruth 3:4," *Jamieson, Fausset, and Brown Commentary*, PC Study Bible V5, (Biblesoft, Inc., 1988-2013).

7 Wiersbe, "Ruth submitted to Boaz. (Ruth 3:6-9)."

8 Adam Clarke, "Ruth 4:1," *Adam Clarke's Commentary*, PC Study Bible V5, (Biblesoft, Inc., 1988-2013).

9 Albert Barnes, "Ruth 4:2," *Barnes' Notes*, PC Study Bible V5, (Biblesoft, Inc., 1988-2013).

10 *Aesop*, Brainy Quotes, <http://www.brainyquote.com/quotes/authors/a/aesop.html>. 2 Jan. 2014.

11 *Mark Twain*, Brainy Quotes, <http://www.brainyquote.com/quotes/authors/m/mark_twain.html>. 2 Jan. 2014.

Chapter 8

1 David Boroff, New York Daily News, <http://www.nydailynews.com/news/national/valedictorian-cut-mentioning-god-graduation-speech-article-1.1369065>. 11 June 2013.

2 *High School Valedictorian Recites Lord's Prayer At Graduation In Defiance Of Prayer Ban*, The Huffington Post, <http://www.huffingtonpost.com/2013/06/05/high-school-valedictorian-prayer_n_3391963.html.> 6 June 2013.

3 *Neil Simon*, Brainy Quotes, <http://www.brainyquote.com/quotes/authors/n/neil_simon.html>. 2 Jan. 2014.

4 Wikianswers.com, <http://wiki.answers.com/Q/How_many_times_does_the_word servant_occur_in_the_Bible#slide=2&article=How_many_times_does_the_word_servant_occur_in_the_Bible>. 2 Jan. 2014.

Chapter 9

1 Warren W. Wiersbe, "A nationwide drought (1 Kings 17:1)," *The Bible Exposition Commentary: Old Testament*, PC Study Bible V5, (Biblesoft, Inc., 1988-2013).

2 John H. Walton, Victor H. Matthews, and Mark W. Chavalas, *The IVP Bible Background Commentary: Old Testament*, (Downers Grove, Ill.: InterVarsity Press, 2000) 377-378.

3 Albert Barnes, "1 Kings 18:21," *Barnes' Notes*, PC Study Bible V5, (Biblesoft, Inc., 1988-2013).

4 Warren W. Wiersbe, "Elijah and Baal (vv.17-29)," *Wiersbe's Expository Outlines on the Old Testament*, PC Study Bible V5, (Biblesoft, Inc., 1988-2013).

5 Thomas Nelson, "Gods, pagan," *Nelson's Illustrated Bible Dictionary*, PC Study Bible V5, (Biblesoft, Inc., 1988-2013).

6 Walton, Matthews, and Chavalas, 378.

7 Barnes, "1 Kings 18:28."

8 Walton, Matthews, and Chavalas, 379.

Chapter 10

1 Charles Swindoll, *Living Above the Level of Mediocrity*, (Nashville, Tenn.: Thomas Nelson 1990), 150ff.

2 John H. Walton, Victor H. Matthews, and Mark W. Chavalas, *The IVP Bible Background Commentary: Old Testament*, (Downers Grove, Ill.: InterVarsity Press, 2000) 390.

3 Walton, Matthews, and Chavalas, 390-391.

4 Walton, Matthews, and Chavalas, 391.

Chapter 11

1 Allison Wachtel, "How Coffins Work," *The Hanging Coffins of the Bo*, <http://science.howstuffworks.com/science-vs-myth/afterlife/coffin4.htm>. 2 Jan. 2014.

2 Heather Whipps, "Top 10 Weird Ways We Deal With the Dead," *Tree Burials*, <http://www.livescience.com/11366-top-10-weird-ways-deal-dead.html>. 2 Jan. 2014.

3 Eternal Reefs, <http://www.eternalreefs.com/>. 2 Jan. 2014.

4 Cryonics Institute, <http://www.cryonics.org/>. 2 Jan. 2014.

5 Delbert Roy Hillers, "Burial in the Bible," <http://www.jewishvirtuallibrary.org/jsource/judaica/ejud_0002_0004_0_03747.html>. 2 Jan. 2014.

6 *Ketef Hinnom*, Arcalog, http://www.arcalog.com/?p=1925. 30 Nov. 2014.

7 Matthew George Easton, "Elisha," *Easton's Bible Dictionary*, PC Study Bible V5, (Biblesoft, Inc., 1988-2013).

8 Albert Barnes, "2 Kings 13:20," *Barnes' Notes*, PC Study Bible V5, (Biblesoft, Inc., 1988-2013).

9 John Meunier, "Fred Rogers at the Television Hall of Fame," <http://johnmeunier.wordpress.com/2008/11/28/fred-rogers-at-the-television-hall-of-fame/>. 2 Jan. 2014.

Chapter 12

1 Adam Clarke, "2 Kings 21:1," *Adam Clarke's Commentary*, PC Study Bible V5, (Biblesoft, Inc., 1988-2013).

2 Clarke, "2 Kings 21:10."

3 Warren W. Wiersbe, "Manasseh-humiliated by affliction (2 Kings 21:1-18; 2 Chronicles 33:1-20)," *The Bible Exposition Commentary: Old Testament*, PC Study Bible V5, (Biblesoft, Inc., 1988-2013).

4 Andrew Robert Fausset, "Manasseh," *Fausset's Bible Dictionary*, PC Study Bible V5, (Biblesoft, Inc., 1988-2013).

5 Fausset.

6 Matthew George Easton, "Manasseh," *Easton's Bible Dictionary*, PC Study Bible V5, (Biblesoft, Inc., 1988-2013).

Chapter 13

1 Amanda Mikelberg and Joe Kemp, New York Daily News, <http://www.nydaily news.com/new-york/generosity-immortalized-photo-article-1.1210565>. 29 Nov. 2012.

2 Thomas Nelson, "Jeremiah," *Nelson's Illustrated Bible Dictionary*, PC Study Bible V5, (Biblesoft, Inc., 1988-2013).

3 Nelson, "Chaldeans."

4 Albert Barnes, "Jeremiah 38:6," *Barnes' Notes*, PC Study Bible V5, (Biblesoft, Inc., 1988-2013).

5 Roswell Dwight Hitchcock, "Ebed-melech," *Hitchcock's Bible Names Dictionary*, PC Study Bible V5, (Biblesoft, Inc., 1988-2013).

6 Matthew Henry, "Jeremiah Put Into the Dungeon; Ebed-melech's Care of Jeremiah. (B.C. 589.)," *Matthew Henry's Commentary on the Whole Bible*, PC Study Bible V5, (Biblesoft, Inc., 1988-2013).

7 Andrew Robert Fausset, "Ebed-melech," *Fausset's Bible Dictionary*, PC Study Bible V5, (Biblesoft, Inc., 1988-2013).

CPSIA information can be obtained at www.ICGtesting.com
Printed in the USA
LVOW10s0503280115

424549LV00001B/1/P